Twentieth Century Art

by Michael Batterberry

Foreword by Howard Conant
New York University

McGRAW-HILL BOOK COMPANY
New York · San Francisco · Toronto

Also in the Discovering Art Series:

CHINESE & ORIENTAL ART adapted by Michael Batterberry
17th & 18th CENTURY ART adapted by Ariane Ruskin
NINETEENTH CENTURY ART adapted by Ariane Ruskin

Acknowledgment is hereby given to Purnell & Sons, Ltd., for the right to base this work on the text of the magazine series "Discovering Art," and to Fratelli Fabbri Editori for the right to make adaptations from the Italian text of *Capolavori Nei Secoli.*

TWENTIETH CENTURY ART
Illustrations copyright © 1961–1964, 1969 by Fratelli Fabbri Editori, Milan, Italy. No part of this work may be reproduced without the permission of the publisher.

Library of Congress Catalog Card Number: 70-76821

FOREWORD

by Howard Conant, *Professor and Chairman, Department of Art Education; and Head, Division of Creative Arts, New York University*

THE STYLE and content of Michael Batterberry's adaptation of *Twentieth Century Art* is as provocative and elucidating as the brilliant, staccato-beat manifestos of the futurists, surrealists, and others described in his text. Augmented by a large and very fine collection of color illustrations, Mr. Batterberry's treatment of the visual arts of the twentieth century is praiseworthy both for its excellent content and the contemporary sparkle of its style.

Traditional art historians often look upon modern artists as old-fashioned adults look upon modern youth: with dismay or with a lack of understanding. Mr. Batterberry's orientation is antithetical to that of the traditional historian; yet his scholarship is impeccable and he never reverts to the unpleasant practice of building a case for one art period at the expense of another. Most histories of art pay little more than lip service to modern art, if indeed they include it at all. Mr. Batterberry not only gives the artists and art works of this century the thoughtful attention they deserve; but he has produced one of the best-written, best-illustrated, and most comprehensive critical histories of twentieth-century art in the category of comprehensive period texts.

One of the most appealing characteristics of *Twentieth Century Art* is its in-depth analysis of major styles, schools, movements, and individual artists' works, accompanied in most cases by several large, full-color illustrations. Readers will be pleased to find that volumes in the "Discovering Art Series" thoughtfully avoid the encyclopedic boredom of art books which mention everything but tell and illustrate little or nothing. *Twentieth Century Art* is, in fact, a substantial volume, and it does provide ample opportunity for the author to deal with little-known but nevertheless important art movements and styles such as the "Section d'Or," "Peintres Maudits," "Jugendstil," and "Intimism."

Speaking of "youth style" (Jugendstil), Mr. Batterberry's book has plenty of it. Readers are bound to read his accounts of the lives of rebellious, impatient, and talented young people with fixed interest. Also interesting is the fact that these rebellious, often misunderstood, youngsters bore such names as Picasso and Modigliani. But even more worthy of consideration is the fact that these anti-social, rebellious youngsters produced, both during their youth and in later years, some of the greatest artistic masterworks of the twentieth century. Like some of today's youthful rebels, Picasso, Modigliani, and their friends were "turned on," highly productive radicals rather than "turned off" indolents.

Mr. Batterberry's *Twentieth Century Art* is admirably suited as a text for art survey and humanities courses. To choose a less profound, less comprehensive, and less well-illustrated text for such courses would certainly be ill advised. *Twentieth Century Art* will make a valuable and interesting addition to the home library; but better still would be individual acquisitions of the entire "Discovering Art Series." Needless to say, the same recommendation applies to school and community libraries.

CONTENTS

2. *Portrait of Ambroise Vollard,*
by Paul Cézanne

Gogh. It suggests that his distorted images (Plate 3), which vibrate with a frantic life and color, were meant to express a strong emotion that would make the viewer *feel* along with the artist, rather than just *see*. In this subjective aim, Van Gogh differed from the impressionists, who, regardless of their rebellious attitudes, sought primarily to capture a visual experience in terms of natural light and color. Deep sentiments were generally ignored by them, in favor of fleeting impressions that would leave the viewer pleased and comfortably undisturbed (Plate 4). How different from the tortured paintings of the Norwegian Edvard Munch. His typically gloomy *Summer Night at Oslofjord* (Plate 5) must definitely be considered expressionistic. A forlorn, solitary little figure that is suggested by two or three brushstrokes, some animate and menacing

trees, and the horrendous mouthlike island in the background all help to communicate an extremely sinister and lonely feeling.

Gauguin called himself a "symbolist." Basically, the term "symbolism" denotes that one thing suggests, recalls, or represents another. Symbols themselves can take innumerable forms. They may be as familiar and obvious as the skull and crossbones on a bottle of poison or as spiritual as the dove representing the Holy Ghost. The symbolism of various colors is so widely accepted that their meanings are taken for granted: for example, the direct association between the white bridal gown and purity, the red rose and love, and the black veil and sorrow. (It should be noted that color symbolism may vary from one culture or era to another.) Moreover, each of us has personal reactions to colors, shapes, or situations, and thus we come to form our own private associations. The painters known as symbolists used such personal symbols in form and color, to convey particular moods or private visions to others.

Gauguin's symbolism consisted of using color freely (that is, boldly and subjectively) rather than realistically. "What beautiful ideas," he exulted, "can be conjured up by form and color, now that we have no religious painting." He argued that, if one wished to paint a beautiful tree, why not use the most pure and brilliant green to represent it? In other words, why dull a bright color straight from the tube by mixing it with another simply to imitate nature? One thinks of a tree as being green, so let it be the most arresting and undiluted hue.

3. *Portrait of Doctor Gachet,* by Vincent van Gogh

4. *Water Lilies,* by Claude Monet

5. *Summer Night at Oslofjord,*
by Edvard Munch

Nevermore (Plate 6), which takes its title and the watchful bird from Edgar Allen Poe's poem "The Raven," bears out these ideas, notwithstanding the painting's deliberately somber tones. Of this picture Gauguin wrote, "I have tried to suggest a certain bygone barbaric luxury in a single nude. . . . It is neither silk nor velvet nor batiste nor gold that creates this luxurious quality, but simply a richness created by the hand of the artist." Among the many artists influenced by the freedom of Gauguin's color and the flatly patterned surfaces of his pictures were Picasso and Henri Matisse (1869–1954).

Another important symbolist, Odilon Redon, frequently used a broad range of shimmering color to create a fantasy world of flowers, winged horses, mysterious men in the moon, and mythological beings. Even in the delicate and relatively straightforward *Portrait of the Artist's Son Ari* (Plate 7), one is struck by an indefinable and haunting air of unreality. It is this visionary or dreamlike quality of Redon's art which foreshadows a later movement called "surrealism."

Van Gogh, Gauguin, and Cézanne shared admirable traits of uncommon artistic integrity and courage. A degree of recognition finally came to Cézanne during his lifetime, but the earlier years of rejection by critics and public had by then left him painfully scarred. Gauguin died in lonely squalor, after having tried vainly to commit suicide in the jungle. Van Gogh, who never found a public during his life, was finally driven mad

6. *Nevermore,* by Paul Gauguin

7. *Portrait of the Artist's Son Ari,* by Odilon Redon

with desperation and shot himself. Yet their dedication to painting never faltered, and they exemplified the French poet Baudelaire's definition of the true artist, who "is responsible to no one but himself. He donates to the centuries to come only his works; he stands surely for himself alone. He dies without issue. He was his own king, his own priest, and his own God." What these three influential figures donated to the next generations will be clearly seen in the ensuing development of expressionism, cubism, symbolism, and various phases of abstract painting.

Matisse and the Fauves

In 1903 a group that included some young avant-garde painters (literally "advance guard," but loosely meaning "ahead of the times") banded together and founded the Société du Salon d'Automne[1]; their intention was to organize group exhibits where artistic freedom would be not only permitted but encouraged. Two years later, one of their showings created a major scandal in Paris. What gave offense, in particular, was one room filled with outrageous paintings by a certain Henri Matisse and his colleagues. The primary colors—red, yellow, and blue—screamed at each other from every wall. The eye was assaulted by orange fields, purple streets, and the portrait of a woman with a bright green line splitting her face. Traditional perspective had been twisted and wrenched into impossible contortions. These must be madmen! No, snickered the noted art critic Louis Vauxcelles, they are "wild beasts." Ever since, the painters of this group have been known as the Fauves (from the French for "wild beasts").

As usual the public thought it was witnessing something entirely without precedent, something entirely new that was obviously intended as a personal insult to its taste and sense of propriety. This is too often the case when the public comes face to face with a revolutionary movement in art. Ironically, these movements are rarely as revolutionary as they might at first seem. Fauvism was no exception; it had not been invented overnight. The best way to describe its gradual emergence would be to follow the career of Henri Matisse, since it was he who led the group—by example, however, rather than being their chosen leader.

Matisse was born into a respectable middle class family at Le Cateau-Cambrésis in 1869. Following his father's wishes, he studied law. However, he suffered a serious illness at the age of twenty, and during his convalescence he took up painting, an activity that changed his entire life. Three years later, despite his father's protests, he entered a Parisian art school, the Académie Julien, where the students were permitted to paint and draw as they wished. Cézanne, Van Gogh, and Toulouse-Lautrec had studied there before him. The following year found him at the official art academy of Paris, the École des Beaux-Arts, where the teaching was severely disciplined and traditional. Fortunately, Matisse was able to enter the classes of Gustave Moreau, where he met such other budding masters as Georges Rouault (1871–1958) and Albert Marquet (1875–1947). Moreau, a symbolist painter best known for his jewel-toned pictures with a strong Oriental flavor, was not a progressive teacher; nevertheless, he was an excellent one, who encouraged his students to develop their own styles by studying the old masters until they knew what they wanted to take from them. This attitude suited Matisse perfectly, and he became passionately interested in such older French masters as Nicolas Poussin, Philippe de Champaigne, and Jean Baptiste Chardin, the country's greatest painter of still life in the eighteenth century. But in later years, Matisse said of this period, "The teachers at the Beaux-Arts used to say to their pupils 'copy nature stupidly.' Throughout my career I have reacted against this attitude, to which I could not submit; my struggle gave rise to various changes of

[1] Among the founders of the Salon were Renoir, Vuillard, Marquet, and Rouault.

course, during which I searched for means of expression beyond the literal copying—such as divisionism and Fauvism."[2]

Matisse's admiration of Cézanne's structural genius was such that he spent his wife's meager dowry on one of the older master's small pictures of bathers. Though the couple could ill afford it then, the Cézanne remained Matisse's proudest possession, and he later claimed that it had provided him with thirty-five years of inspiration. But it was color that appealed to Matisse more than anything else, and for a time he boldly experimented with divisionist color techniques. [Compare, for instance, Seurat's *Seine at the Grand Jatte* with Matisse's *Luxury, Peace, and Voluptuousness* (Plates 8, 9).] Matisse also learned much from the expressive, emotional color of Van Gogh and Gauguin. Gauguin's insistence on the artist's right to paint any object the color he *felt* it to be liberated Matisse further. In 1898

8. *The Seine at the Grande Jatte,* by Georges Seurat

Matisse painted a bright blue male nude, which left even his most understanding friends speechless. He theorized that "Simple [pure] colors can act upon the inner feelings with all the more force because they are simple. A blue, for instance, accompanied by the shimmer of its complimentaries, acts upon the feelings like a sharp blow on a gong. The same with red and yellow, and the artist must be able to sound them when he needs to."

Matisse was equally experimental and daring in composing a picture's overall design in relation to its edges: "The whole arrangement of my picture is expressive. The place occupied by the figures or objects, the empty spaces around them, the proportions, everything plays a part. Composition is the art of arranging in a decorative manner the various elements at the painter's disposal for the expression of his feelings."

Matisse absorbed the ideas of any and all artists who interested him, including those of the Middle East, and in this way gradually arrived at the point of realizing how his ideal painting should look. Like Cézanne, Matisse wanted to emphasize the existence of a painting as something complete in itself, with a life all its own. He wanted to create pictures that paraphrased nature rather than to copy it "stupidly," for it is impossible to reproduce nature exactly. No paint can ever be as brilliant as the most brilliant natural light. Matisse himself said, "Never struggle with nature to reproduce light; we must look for an equivalent . . . for the

---

[2] "Divisionism" refers to a theoretic method of painting invented by the neoimpressionist painter Georges Seurat (1859–1891). As an art historical term, "neoimpressionist" was assigned specifically to Seurat and his group. In essence, divisionism (also called "pointillism") meant the scientific breaking down of areas into tiny contrasting spots of pure color that, owing to laws of optics, blur into vibrant solid hues when seen from a distance. Seurat's technique differed from the impressionists' portrayal of flickering light in that he followed an almost purely mathematical procedure.

9. *Luxury, Peace, and Voluptuousness,* by Henri Matisse

means we use are in themselves dead. Otherwise we would inevitably be led to place the sun behind the canvas."

Light indicates space. We would find it difficult to judge distances with any accuracy were it not for the light falling on objects as they recede toward the horizon. Matisse understood, as many artists had, that certain colors suggest space and light more than others. Warm colors (red is the strongest) appear to advance toward the viewer, and cold colors such as blues and greens to recede. Colors in the distance are more muted than those in the foreground. Why not, then, suggest light and space purely in terms of their color characteristics? All

these ideas were brought together in Matisse's paintings, with his most frequent themes being figures in interior settings and still life (Plate 10). Other painters interested in these same problems were soon inspired to follow his lead.

The painters who exhibited in the original gallery of Fauves included four other ex-students of Gustave Moreau at the École des Beaux-Arts: Albert Marquet, Georges Rouault, Charles Camoin (1879–   ), and Henri Manguin (1874–1943). Matisse met Marquet, Camoin, and Manguin at school and often went sketching with them at the Louvre and in the streets of Paris. Gradually the fellow students began to paint in a

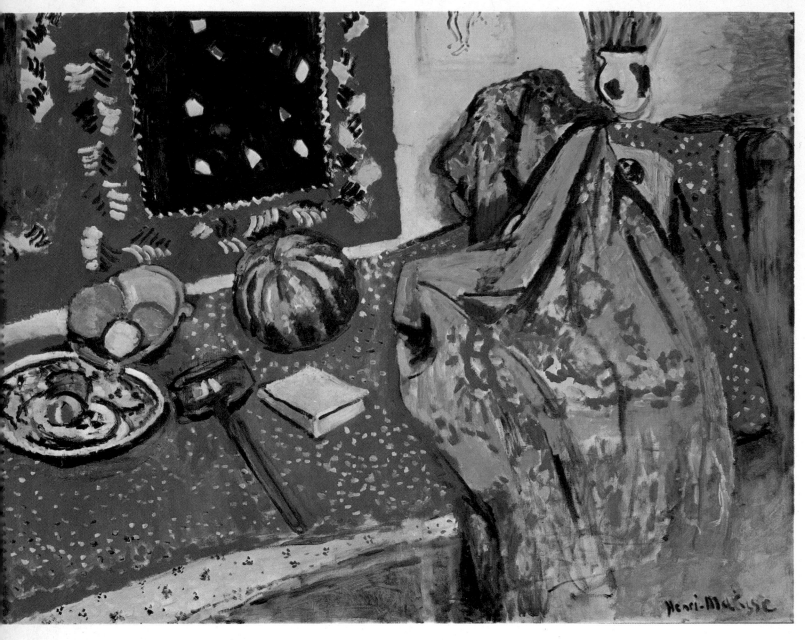

10. *Still Life,* by Henri Matisse

similar manner. Marquet's pictures, however, show an undeniable attachment to the impressionists in his fondness for sparkling beach and street scenes. Only his bold use of pure color puts him in the general category of the Fauves. Examples of this are the flags and deep orange faces of the sailors in *The Beach at Fécamp* and the sunny primary colors of the billboards in *Posters at Trouville* (Plates 11, 12).

Manguin's experiments with using color

to suggest both direct and reflected light were more adventurous than Marquet's. In *Woman at the Window* (Plate 13), he has used a whole range of yellows, mauves, reds, and greens to give the effect of strong outdoor light falling on the shadowy figure of his model.

In 1901 this circle of friends was joined by André Derain (1880–1954) and Maurice Vlaminck (1876–1958), who were professional athletes turned artists. They shared a studio and had developed similar painting styles. Vlaminck—bicycle racer, violinist, lover of bargemen's cafés, speed, and music halls—was born in Paris of Flemish parents. Van Gogh was his idol; in fact, Vlaminck claimed that he was more important to him than his own father. This is even more evident in *Gardens at Châtou* than in *The Village* (Plates 14, 15). Vlaminck was the soul of spontaneity, of wild expressiveness and joyous life. In these qualities he typifies most fully the spirit of Fauvism.

Derain was influenced by Vlaminck,

Matisse, Seurat, and the divisionists. The influence of the last-named was to be seen particularly in the treatment of sky and water in two London-inspired paintings, *Westminister Bridge* and *Blackfriars* (Plates 16, 17). His colors and compositions leap with life and activity, yet are always carefully balanced. Both Vlaminck and Derain later fell under the spell of Cézanne's paintings. At this time, Vlaminck modified the brilliantly expressive daubs of color he used to portray a dancer at the notorious Paris nightclub Le Rat Mort ("The Dead Rat")

11. *The Beach at Fécamp,* by Albert Marquet

12. *Posters at Trouville,* by Albert Marquet

13. *Woman at the Window,* by Henri Manguin

14. *Gardens at Châtou,* by Maurice Vlaminck

15. *The Village,* by Maurice Vlaminck

16. *Westminster Bridge,* by André Derain

17. *Blackfriars,* by André Derain

18. *Dancer at "Le Rat Mort,"*
by Maurice Vlaminck

for such serenely structured, more somber-colored studies as *The Old Harbor, Marseilles* (Plates 18, 19).

All these young artists banded together and exhibited at various shows around Paris, which in turn attracted new followers. The Dutchman Kees van Dongen (1877–1968) joined them, and in 1904 their ranks were swelled by three painters from the port of Le Havre who had come under Matisse's influence: Othon Friesz (1879–1949), Raoul Dufy (1877–1953), and Georges Braque (1882–1963). Upon Matisse's suggestion, Friesz divorced himself from his original impressionist tendencies and began to study carefully the paintings of Van Gogh and Seurat, which made him realize that he "could obtain the equivalent of sunlight by a technique based on orchestrated colors and emotional transpositions of nature, and that nature yields her secrets to passionate search and enthusiasm." His own passionate search led Friesz to paint vibrant pictures full of dancing light, a fine example being his *Portrait of Fernand Fleuret* (Plate 20).

As we shall see later, Dufy's personal style was to become extremely individual and easy to identify in the years following his association with the Fauves. A faint indication of what was to evolve can be noted in *Harbor of Le Havre* (Plate 21). The large, clearly defined areas of contrasting color (as seen in the water) would in the future serve him as flat compositional backgrounds bearing no logical relationship of form to the drawings superimposed on them. Struck by

19. *The Old Harbor, Marseilles,*
by Maurice Vlaminck

20. *Portrait of Fernand Fleuret,* by Othon Friesz

21. *Harbor of Le Havre,* by Raoul Dufy

Matisse's simplified color, Dufy passed through a transitional period as a Fauve, during which he painted boldly festive scenes such as *Decorated Streets* and *The Three Umbrellas* (Plates 22, 23).

Van Dongen's most important and un-mannered work dates from the Fauve era. (It should be noted here that there was no Fauvist *period* or *school* proper; nor were the

22. *Decorated Streets,* by Raoul Dufy

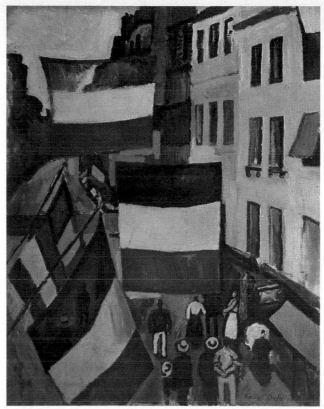

23. *The Three Umbrellas,* by Raoul Dufy

Fauves committed to any strict set of self-imposed rules or theories.) Van Dongen's Fauvism is best expressed in the exuberant color and brushstrokes of *Liverpool Nightclub* (Plate 24). Nowadays his name usually brings to mind sophisticated portraits of international beauties with bobbed hair and silent film star eye makeup. This sort of stylish picture, such as his *Marchesa Casati* (Plate 25), ensured him a wide and wealthy patronage, if not permanent critical success. Nevertheless, even at their trickiest, Van Dongen's portraits retained some Fauve traits, such as the Marchesa's ultramarine blue hound.

Georges Braque's involvement with Fauvism could be called a serious "flirtation." A quiet, intelligent giant of a man, he adopted new techniques with amazing facility and understanding. His physical strength was impressive. The American avant-garde writer and art collector Gertrude Stein noted that Braque was always counted on to help hang the heaviest paintings, and that singlehandedly he had prevented two hefty statues from toppling on the guests when a banquet at Picasso's studio got out of control. It was with Picasso, too, that Braque would firmly establish his reputation as the codeveloper of cubism.

24. *Liverpool Nightclub,* by Kees van Dongen

25. *Marchesa Casati,* by Kees van Dongen

26. *Houses at L'Estaque,* by Georges Braque

With the exception of Matisse, Braque approached the art of Cézanne the most wisely. In 1908 Braque and Dufy traveled to L'Estaque, the Provençal region where Cézanne had so frequently painted. There Braque was able to see with his own eyes what had helped to inspire Cézanne's ideas concerning form and space (Plate 26). Shortly after this experience, Braque and Picasso launched their artistic revolution—a revolution which was to exceed even that of the Fauves in its consequences.

Picasso and Rouault

PABLO PICASSO, the twentieth century's great innovator, was born in 1881 in Málaga, Spain, where his father, also a painter, was a teacher in the School of Arts and Crafts. During Picasso's teens the family moved to Barcelona, where his father again took up teaching. Pablo, who from childhood had given many indications of exceptional talent, entered the Barcelona Academy at the age of fifteen and pursued art studies there for several years. It has already been noted that his first actual contact with Parisian life came in 1900 at the Art Nouveau–influenced World's Fair. He was affected not only by this style but also by Toulouse-Lautrec, Gauguin, and a group called the Nabis.

The Nabis took their name from the Hebrew word meaning "prophet" or "seer." Their leader Paul Sérusier gathered this group together in Paris after returning from Brittany, where he had been closely associated with yet another group led by Gauguin at Pont-Aven. Like Gauguin, the Nabis rejected naturalism. Two of the most talented, Pierre Bonnard (1867–1947) and Edouard Vuillard (1868–1940), had a studio together and shared the same general ideas about painting. Their preferred subjects were domestic scenes composed of contrasting flat patterns and luminous color effects. Because of its intimate quality, the name "intimism" has been given to their style of painting. Bonnard was also fascinated by the idea of showing figures in silhouette, as seen in his *Dinner by Lamplight* (Plate 27). The general style of pictures like this derived from Chardin and from certain Dutch genre and still-life masters of the seventeenth century. Both Bonnard and Vuillard wished to give maximum pleasure

and a comfortable satisfaction through their paintings, to create an intimate, yet colorfully expressive world (Plates 28, 29). Among the great masters of the postimpressionist period, they continued to paint until almost the middle of the twentieth century. Bonnard, particularly, remained faithful to his early intimist ideas and style, even when dealing with subjects outside the family circle. In outdoor scenes he was generally more successful in painting the small-scale landscape of gardens rather than broad expanses. He was also adept at depicting such preferred impressionist subjects as people joined in good fellowship or engaged in such pleasant pastimes as sailing (Plate 30). Mealtimes were another favorite theme (Plate 31).

Bonnard had a rare ability that was not always found in the Fauves: he could use extremely bright and vivid colors to create a subtle instead of a harsh effect. Above all, he was able to bring a profound sense of humanity to his intimate domestic scenes.

The Flower Seller (Plate 32) was painted by Picasso in 1901, when he was twenty; in many ways it recalls a series of paintings done by Bonnard a few years earlier. By 1903 he had advanced sufficiently in his own direction to paint the overwhelming picture *Life* (Plate 33). Picasso's life-long concern for humanity dominates this phase of his career, which is known as the "Blue period" (roughly 1901–1904). The couple to the left in *Life* represents the values of love and marriage, while the woman and baby represent motherhood and the eternal cycles of life. The pictures on the wall portray anguish and loneliness. The paintings of the Blue period, with their predominant cool tones of blue and blue-green, usually dwell on sad or desolate people—blindmen, beg-

27. *Dinner by Lamplight,* by Pierre Bonnard

gars, the hopelessly poor. These figures, which are elongated, angular, and frequently as fleshless as skeletons, often sit drooping with a kind of painful grace over bleak tables (Plate 34).

The pathetic clowns that recur as themes during Picasso's Blue period also appear in the powerful, evocative paintings of Georges Rouault. The art critic James Thrall Soby neatly summed up Rouault as "a solitary figure in an era of group manifestoes and shared directions . . . an artist with a limited vision of unlimited fecundity in contrast to many other leading painters who have scanned and pivoted but seldom stared fixedly for long. . . ." Rouault, a devout Catholic, painted religious scenes at a time when this kind of subject matter had generally been abandoned by others. An emotional and moral man, he expressed his outrage at vice, hypocrisy, and corruption in rich color as brilliant as the finest stained glass. On occasion, these pictures provoked outrage on the part of their viewers which was as intense as that which had prompted their creation; even some of Rouault's

28. *Dining Room Overlooking the Garden,*
by Pierre Bonnard

closest friends were profoundly shocked by such paintings of unattractive nudes as his *At the Mirror* (Plate 35). On the other hand, his compassion for mankind could be as touchingly expressed as in his sad, weary portrait *The Apprentice Worker* (Plate 36). Along with his stained-glass colors, the powerful black contour lines of *The Passion* and the flirtatious *Carmencita* (Plates 37, 38), both painted in Rouault's old age, were his trademark. It would not be stretching the point to compare Rouault's strong, structural outlines with the dark lead strips used in stained-glass windows. Therefore, it comes as no surprise to discover that Rouault had completed his apprenticeship to a stained-glass maker even before entering Gustave Moreau's studio at the Beaux-Arts in 1892. Moreau became a second father to him. Before that, his grandfather ("who loved the fine arts—but outside official

29. *The Newspaper,* by Edouard Vuillard

30. *Signac and Friends Boating,*
by Pierre Bonnard

31. *Dessert,* by Pierre Bonnard

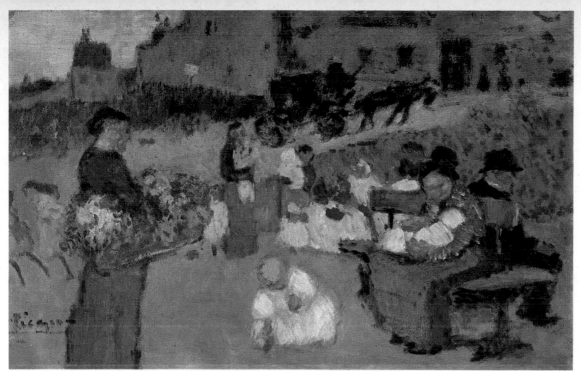

32. *The Flower Seller,* by Pablo Picasso

33. *Life,* by Pablo Picasso

circles") was his sole spiritual support. One of Rouault's earliest memories was of drawing larger-than-life-size heads in chalk on his grandfather's polished wood floors for the old man's pleasure. His grandfather often spoke of artistic integrity and independence, and the impression these talks made went bone deep. Toward the end of his life Rouault declared, "I must say, without boasting too much about it, that I have practiced this often legendary art with more or less luck; I have respected a certain internal order and laws which I hope are traditional; removed from passing fashions and contemporaries—critics, artists, and dealers—I believe I have kept my spiritual liberty."

34. *The Blindman,* by Pablo Picasso

Picasso said that, on the whole, people looked at pictures blindly, stupidly, as they had been told to or thought they should, "instead of trying to sense what inner life there was in the men who painted them." This is a good statement to keep in mind. He added, "A picture is not thought out and settled beforehand. While it is being done it changes as one's thoughts change. And when it is finished, it still goes on changing, according to the state of mind of whoever is looking at it. A picture lives a life like a living creature, undergoing the changes imposed on us by our life from day to day. This is natural enough, as the picture lives only through the man who is looking at it."

That Picasso's thoughts were changing in 1904 becomes evident with the advent of his "Rose period." The colors of his new paintings were predominantly pink, yellow ocher, and gray. Strolling players, acrobats, clowns, and harlequins replaced blind and destitute people as his subjects. Picasso had moved to Paris and set up a studio in Montmartre in a creaky old building nick-named the "Bateau-Lavoir" (the French name for a clumsy boat from which laun-dresses used to wash clothes in the Seine). There he formed a circle of close friends

35. *At the Mirror* (detail), by Georges Rouault

37. *The Passion,* by Georges Rouault

38. *Carmencita,* by Georges Rouault

including the poet, critic, and promoter of experimental art Guillaume Apollinaire and the poet Max Jacob. They made the atmosphere electric with their brilliant artistic debates. The young painter Marie Laurencin (1885–1956), who was Apollinaire's constant companion, later recalled: "The evening he [Apollinaire] usually spent at Picasso's place, 13 rue Ravignan, in company with Max Jacob, and the three of them did nothing but quarrel, catch each other out, glare at each other, and, most of all, exchange curses, which was their speciality; after which they would be idolising one another all over the place."

Everyone and anyone was welcome at Picasso's table, even if there were only a couple of chairs and barely enough money

36. *The Apprentice Worker,* by Georges Rouault

39. *Family of Saltimbanques,* by Pablo Picasso

to buy macaroni and mineral water. Montmartre had long been familiar with wild and uproarious Bohemians, and this new generation did nothing to let the old legends die. Near the Bateau-Lavoir were the old mills that had been converted into gay and noisily informal nightclubs, as well as a charming old-fashioned circus, whose performers Picasso idealized in his Rose period paintings (Plate 39). Picasso later dismissed this enchantingly graceful period of subtle colors and refined drawing in his career by declaring "All that was just sentiment."

In 1906, Picasso returned to Spain for the summer. There he renewed contact with Spanish Gothic sculpture and, more important, with ancient Iberian sculpture dating back to the time before the Roman Empire. Early Iberian sculpture has a stark and simple strength and unrefined, unconventional proportions, to the point of appearing primitive.

The word "primitive" has several uses and misuses in art. In one sense it can be applied to the art of primitive societies, such as tribal masks and totems. "Primitive" can also be applied to so-called "naïve" (*naïf*) art, as created by self-taught artists such as Grandma Moses or Henri Rousseau (1844–1910). The Douanier Rousseau (the French *douanier* means "customs inspector"), who exhibited with the Fauves among others, because of his fantastic jungle scenes sometimes is incorrectly labeled "primitive" in both senses. His uncomplicated *Still Life* (Plate 40), painted with deceptively amateurish simplicity, clearly shows that he was a primitive of the second, self-taught category. Ironically, Rousseau's intention

40. *Still Life,* by Henri Rousseau

was never deliberately to distort but, hopefully, to paint like the great artists whose work he admired in the Louvre. We shall return to the other classification of "primitive" in our discussion of the German expressionists and of the celebrated Picasso painting that led to the development of cubism.

Under the influence of the Iberian sculpture, Picasso abandoned his Rose period and experimented in a ruggedly simplified new style, as evidenced in his *Self-portrait* (Plate 41). Such works, along with his introduction to African sculpture by Matisse, led to the revolutionary *Les Demoiselles d'Avignon* (Plate 42). This picture is essentially an arrangement of figures, but its similarity to anything ever painted before begins and ends there. The background draperies have been flattened and violently broken up into geometric planes with a life all their own; the color, though limited in range, is peculiarly dazzling.

Les Demoiselles d'Avignon is a perfect illustration of Picasso's statement that a picture changes along with the painter's thoughts. All that remains of the original conception is the small arrangement of fruit at the bottom of the canvas. All five faces were at one point rendered in the Iberian-influenced style of the three on the left. The two unsettling masklike heads on the right were painted in following Picasso's sudden fascination with African primitive art. The importance of this painting was not immediately recognized by Braque, Matisse, and Derain, though none denied its harsh expressive power. It has been written about this influential work: "But it marked, none the less, the end of 500 years of tradition. A painting was no longer three-dimensional, inviting one back through a 'window' into a different world; instead space and form were manipulated

41. *Self-portrait,* by Pablo Picasso

43. *Seated Nude,* by Pablo Picasso

42. *Les Demoiselles d'Avignon,* by Pablo Picasso

44. *The Aficionado,* by Pablo Picasso

by the artist on the two-dimensional picture plane. It is from such an achievement that the development of cubism proceeded."

A memorial exhibition of Cézanne in 1907 inspired Picasso to delve even deeper into the possibilities of handling formal structure and space. Cézanne's advice to treat nature in terms of the cylinder, the sphere, and the cone was adopted by Picasso not only for landscape but for still life and figures as well. By 1909–1910, he had progressed as far as the *Seated Nude* (Plate

45. *The Billiard Room*, by Georges Braque

46. *Girl with a Guitar,* by Georges Braque

43). This painting shows how rapidly Picasso, in the company of Braque, raced ahead of Cézanne's pioneer discoveries and opened up a whole new visual world. Realistic detail, atmospheric effects, and naturalistic color were abandoned. Attention was focused on movement in space, on seeing things from diverse angles, and on artistic means rather than on subject matter. Matisse was unmoved and contemptuously referred to these paintings as a jumble of "little cubes." The critic Louis Vauxcelles also used the word "cubist" in describing the fragmented compositions. In reply to his critics, Picasso remarked, "I paint objects as I think them, not as I see them."

Braque and Picasso spent part of the summer of 1912 together at Sorgues, near Avignon. There they took cubism a step further by introducing letters and names into their pictures. Because these were flat components, attention was drawn to the flat surface of the picture. For example, in Picasso's *Aficionado* ("Bullfight Fan"; Plate 44), we see the name of the place where he attended bullfights (Nîmes) and the local newspaper, *Le Toréro.*

Braque called upon his early training as a decorator to introduce such effects as marbling, wood graining, and stencils into his paintings (Plate 45); moreover, both artists began to incorporate bits and pieces of real newspaper and wallpaper into their works (Plates 46, 47). The technique of pasting cutouts onto canvas is called *papier collé*; the term "collage" was used to describe this new art medium of Braque and Picasso. Also, to distinguish the new style from their earlier one ("analytic cubism"), this phase was called "synthetic cubism."

The creation of cubism had proceeded quickly. From the summer of 1909, Braque and Picasso worked as if "roped together

47. *The Violin,* by Pablo Picasso

48. *Nude Figures in a Wood,* by Fernand Léger

like mountaineers," as Braque described it. Their experiments were reaching toward a total grasp of reality, despite any apparent evidence to the contrary. Braque has said, "It was a means of getting closer to objects within the limits that painting would allow. Through fragmentation I was able to establish space and movement in space, and I was unable to introduce objects until after I had created space."

The two most important artists to adopt a cubist style of painting after 1910 were the Frenchman Fernand Léger (1881–1955) and the Spaniard Juan Gris (1887–1927). Others experimented with it with varying degrees of success and impatience, but Léger and Gris developed individual styles of enduring originality.

Léger had been trained as an architect; throughout his career he never completely lost his fascination with machinery and rather cold geometric shapes. He was yet another artist impressed by the Cézanne retrospective in 1907, and by 1910 Léger was painting cubist pictures peopled with robot-like figures, such as his *Nude Figures in a*

Wood (Plate 48). By 1911 he had tilted the picture space to create greater depth and introduced bright contrasting colors into his canvases (Plate 49). The year 1913 saw Léger still boldly advancing in his own industrial-inspired direction. While there is no identifiable subject matter, paintings such as *Contrast of Forms* (Plate 50) suggest a violent modern mechanical activity. Léger was an intelligent man who thoughtfully expressed his feelings about the new art and its place in modern life:

Abstract art is dominated by the same desire for complete freedom and perfection which inspires saints, heroes and madmen. It is a peak on which only a few creative artists and their admirers can maintain themselves. In fact, the very danger of this peak is the rarefied atmosphere by which he is surrounded. Modeling, contrasts, and objects disappear. All that remains are the purest and the most precise of relationships, a few colors, a few lines, some white spaces devoid of depth. Respect for the vertical plane—thin, rigid, limiting. This is the purism: incorruptible. The tumult and the speed of modern life, which is dynamic and full of contrasts, beat furiously against this light and brittle construction as it emerges coldly from the chaos.

49. *Smokers,* by Fernand Léger

Juan Gris took a cool and classical approach to cubism. This penniless little Spaniard arrived in Paris in 1906, and until 1910 he barely kept himself alive by working as a cartoonist. When he returned afterward to serious painting, he developed a disciplined and logically thought-out form of cubism, such as is seen in the severely organized and cool-colored *Still Life with Bottles and a Knife* (Plate 51). Following this phase, Gris experimented with the color and collage of synthetic cubism with truly beautiful results. In these works the contrast between reality and manipulated planes and textures provides great visual interest (Plate 52). Of this style of synthetic cubism Gris said, "I proceed from the general to

50. *Contrast of Forms,* by Fernand Léger

52. *Still Life with Fruit Dish and Water Bottle,*
by Juan Gris

La Section d'Or

AMONG THE other, somewhat less significant followers of cubism were Albert Gleizes (1881–1953) and Jean Metzinger (1883–1956). (See Plates 53 and 54.) Together, in 1912, they published their book *Du Cubisme* ("On Cubism"), which was the first major literary piece to justify cubism. Other contemporary names of note included Robert Delaunay (1885–1941), Roger de la Fresnaye (1885–1925), Louis Marcoussis (1883–1941), and the three Duchamp brothers, who were better known individually as Jacques Villon (1875–1963), Raymond Duchamp-Villon (1876–1918), and Marcel Duchamp (1887–1968). During 1911 the work of this group was represented at three major exhibitions, and in 1912 they added the Salon de la Section d'Or ("Golden Section") to their list.

Among the Section d'Or group, led by Gaston Duchamp (under the pseudonym Jacques Villon), three important tendencies may be detected. The first was the attempt to represent movement. The second was an expanding use of color—a problem that, as you will have noticed, Picasso and Braque deliberately avoided in the early days before synthetic cubism. The third was the carrying of cubism across the threshold into the realm of purely abstract art.

The still lifes of Picasso and Braque dealt with many happy symbols of Bohemian or café life—playing cards, guitars, wine bottles, newspapers, glasses, and violins. But in 1912 a group calling themselves the futurists arrived from Italy, babbling vehemently about the glories of war, speed, power, and violent movement. Taking their cue, Villon attempted in his *Marching Soldiers*

the particular . . . Cézanne turns a bottle into a cylinder, but I begin with a cylinder and create . . . a particular bottle." And of Gris himself, Apollinaire wrote: "Here is the man who has meditated on everything modern, here is the painter who wants to conceive only new structures, whose aim is to draw or paint nothing but materially pure forms."

51. *Still Life with Bottles and a Knife,* by Juan Gris

53. *Women Sewing,* by Albert Gleizes

54. *Still Life,* by Jean Metzinger

(Plate 55) to create the effect of an advancing military column. This subject is represented by jagged patterns suggesting motion rather than by naturalistic figures. His younger brother, Marcel Duchamp, was similarly interested in expressing movement. Duchamp's famous *Nude Descending a Staircase, No. 2* provoked a chorus of outrage when shown at the 1913 Armory Show, New York's first large-scale direct exposure to European modern art. The scandal was prompted not so much by the stated subject matter as by the perplexing way in which it was presented. The general brownish-gold color range of *Le Passage de la Vierge à la Mariée* (Plate 56) is quite similar to that of Duchamp's more notorious work, as is its sense of progression from the upper left-hand corner to the bottom right.

Roger de la Fresnaye used bright, prettily colored planes to add visual interest to his extremely simplified cubistic (but less fragmented) compositions. In the *Seated Man* (Plate 57), the artist's colors suggest gradations of light rather than spatial distinctions.

Robert Delaunay was much more successful in drenching cubism with color. Influenced by Cézanne and early cubism, he originally painted architectural themes; but between 1910 and 1912, he gradually permitted his forms to be dissolved by light

55. *Marching Soldiers,* by Jacques Villon

56. *Le Passage de la Vierge à la Mariée,* by Marcel Duchamp

57. *Seated Man,* by Roger de la Fresnaye

(Plate 58). As he wrote, "The breaking up of form by light creates colored planes. These colored planes are the structure of the picture, and nature is no longer a subject for description but a pretext." The next logical step was to abandon all attempt at realism and step into the colorful harmonies of pure abstract art (Plate 59).

Following in Delaunay's path was the Czech artist Frank (František) Kupka (1871–1957), who evolved an abstract art divorced from realism totally, used as a means of poetic and intellectual expression (Plate 60). Delaunay himself never went quite that far. Even at their most abstract, his paintings were meant to suggest the speed and jerky rhythms of modern life.

Cubism was initially a way of breaking down and rearranging form in terms of two,

58. *Le Manege des Cochons,*
by Robert Delaunay

59. *Oval,* **by Robert Delaunay**

60. *Arrangement in Verticals,* by Frank Kupka

rather than three, dimensions. Nonetheless, its simplifications could be and were applied to sculpture by artists such as Henri Laurens (1885–1954), Alexander Archipenko (1887–1964), Jacques Lipchitz (1891–   ), Henri Gaudier-Brzeska (1891–1915), and Raymond Duchamp-Villon, and by Picasso himself.

The broken surfaces of Picasso's *Head of a Woman* (Plate 61) catch the light with a flickering effect quite like the works of Auguste Rodin, the nineteenth-century French genius who linked older and modern sculpture. But Picasso has distorted and dislocated the facial structure in much the same manner as he did in his cubist paintings.

Henri Laurens' *Portrait of Marthe Girieud* (Plate 62) shows the direct influence of both cubism and the so-called "primitive" arts of Assyria. A sense of earlier primitive art is also found in Alexander Archipenko's small, gracefully swelling bronze *Female Nude* (Plate 63). Archipenko, a Russian who was closely associated with the Salon de la Section d'Or, managed to translate cubism genuinely into sculpture by breaking his

61. *Head of a Woman,* by Pablo Picasso

63. *Female Nude,* by Alexander Archipenko

62. *Portrait of Marthe Girieud,*
by Henri Laurens

surfaces up into brightly colored geometric segments (Plate 64).

The Lithuanian-born sculptor Jacques Lipchitz, about 1913–1914, "felt the necessity to bring more evident order into what nature showed me and which seemed too chaotic. . . . And I started to simplify, to abstract, to take away what did not seem essential." This desire to strip away all but the most essential distinguishing elements can be seen in his *Dancer* (Plate 65).

Raymond Duchamp-Villon was probably the most important of the cubist sculptors. His work was also influenced somewhat by the Italian futurist theories of motion, as his brothers' paintings had been. In studies such as *Horse* (Plate 66), his concentration on movement has produced the simplified planes of a machine that looks as if it could uncoil dangerously at any moment. Gaudier-Brzeska, just before his death in World War I, tried to introduce this style of sculpture to England.

World War I, in which many of the cubists took part (Braque recovered from a bad wound, Apollinaire died of his), signaled the end of the style. Its effects, however, on architecture and design and on our way of looking at the world have been of lasting importance.

64. *Pierrot Carrousel,* by Alexander Archipenko

65. *Dancer,* by Jacques Lipchitz

66. *Horse,* by Raymond Duchamp-Villon

The Futurists

THE MANNER in which Umberto Boccioni's futurist *Unique Forms of Continuity in Space* (Plate 67) is modeled bears distinct similarities to Duchamp-Villon's *Horse* (Plate 66). In this piece of sculpture Boccioni expresses the vigorous, fluid motion of a striding figure. He has said that he was attempting "to model the atmosphere that surrounds things"—a typically futurist project.

What the futurists lacked in numbers they made up for in startling declarations, noisy demonstrations, public meetings, speeches, fights, and widely publicized exhibits in all the major capitals of Europe. The movement, which was made up of young Italian artists, had been initiated by the poet and dramatist Filippo Tommaso Marinetti (1876–1944). These artists felt, with some justification, that for far too long Italy had been content with smugly resting on the laurels of its old masters. They wanted to abolish artistic dependence on the past and to set themselves up as the leaders of contemporary art. For this reason, the name "futurist" was chosen deliberately to provoke both the conservative Italian public and the progressive artists of Paris. In doing so, the Italian artists succeeded in infuriating their own countrymen, but major French artists such as Picasso remained aloof.

The way in which the movement was first announced was also calculated to cause a commotion. The first of the futurist manifestoes, which was concerned with literature, was published on the front page of the respectable Paris newspaper *Le Figaro*, on February 20, 1909. Written by Marinetti, it did not mince words: "We shall sing the love of danger, energy and boldness . . . ," and "we declare that the world's splendor has been enriched by a new beauty, the beauty of speed. A racing motor-car, its hood adorned with great pipes like snakes with explosive breath . . . a roaring motor-car which runs like a machine gun is more beautiful than the Winged Victory of Samothrace." As if this were not sufficiently passionate or unsettling, he fanned the flames even harder: "We wish to glorify War . . . to destroy museums, the libraries." This was not necessarily the ranting of a madman, but a wild poetic outburst by a person who, in all truth, never really appreciated painting.

The futurist movement in Milan was joined in 1909 by three young painters, Umberto Boccioni (1882–1916), Carlo Carrà (1881–1966), and Luigi Russolo

67. *Unique Forms of Continuity in Space,* by Umberto Boccioni

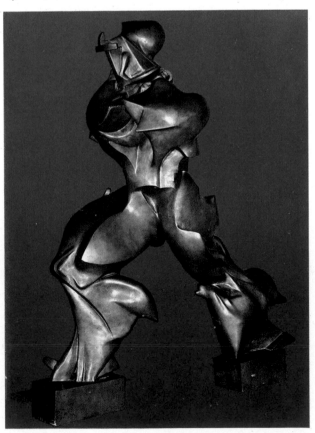

(1885–1947). They combined forces with Gino Severini (1883–1966) and Giacomo Balla (1871–1958), a teacher of both Boccioni and Severini. Together they produced the technical manifesto *La pittura futurista* ("Futurist Painting"), which, before its publication on April 11, 1910, was proclaimed from a theater stage in Turin.

Their arguments were presented logically. First, they stated flatly that their growing need for truth could no longer be satisfied with form and color as these had been understood in the past. Artists should strive to represent dynamic movement and speed by the breaking down of forms and shapes. Like the cubists, they felt that space was the atmosphere around figures and therefore should be given equal attention in painting. But, in theory they went further and insisted that all movement around, as well as space near and far, must be studied as part of what they labeled "universal dynamism." They wanted to "put the spectator in the center of the picture" by realizing the theory that "movement and light destroy the materiality of bodies." Other less important, yet refreshingly unusual ideas included: "Art critics are useless or harmful"; "The name of 'madman' with which it is attempted to gag all innovators should be looked upon as a title of honor"; and finally, "We demand, for ten years, the total suppression of the nude in painting." Their convictions seem particularly outspoken when one learns that, still no paintings had been produced to put these theories into practice.

Of the five painters who had signed the manifesto, Balla, who was exploring the divisionist style in Rome, was perhaps the most established artist. Severini, on the other hand, had lived in Paris since 1906, knew Picasso and Braque, and was well

68. *The Riot in the Galleria,* by Umberto Boccioni

aware of all the latest French artistic developments. He had been using a complicated divisionist technique derived from Seurat's paintings. Both Carrà and Boccioni had painted sentimental pictures in which symbolist influence could be noticed. However, just before the birth of futurism, Boccioni switched styles and adapted divisionism to his gloomy realistic pictures. Russolo, who had received a thorough musical training, was later to become involved as a composer with futurist "noise machines." His painting was essentially self-taught. Each of these painters worked toward his own conception and interpretation of futurism for their first group exhibition in April, 1911.

Boccioni's first notable futurist picture was *The Riot in the Galleria* (Plate 68). At first glance, he seems primarily interested in depicting a fight between two women in front of a café. The artist's real intention

69. Sketch for *The City Rises,* by Umberto Boccioni

70. *States of Mind II* ("Those Who Go"), by Umberto Boccioni

was to express the effect of a surging, hysterical crowd that streams toward the center of the picture, in contrast to the stable vertical lines of the buildings. His divisionist handling of color heightens the feeling of movement and sparkling light. Nevertheless, the spectator has not been put "in the center of the picture" as the manifesto demanded he should. One sees the action as he would in a still photograph outside a movie house; one does not feel involved in the violence.

Boccioni's next major work succeeded more fully in conveying futurist ideals. Before painting it he had said, "I feel I want to paint the new . . . I am nauseated by old walls and old palaces. I want the new, the expressive, the wonderous and wonderful." He found this in the vast construction projects then being undertaken in the suburbs of Milan. He was particularly excited by the huge straining workhorses as appropriate symbols of the new construction. In a series of sketches for the finished picture, which was entitled *The City Rises* (Plate 69), we can see how he "tried for a great synthesis of labor, light and movement." Strenuous activity and extraordinary energy engulfs the spectator and does not let him go. He is in the midst of it all and can feel the wrenching pull of muscle, hear the grunting din of workers and animals, and see the scaffolding rise before his eyes. The slashes of bright color are used in a modified divisionist manner with energetic brilliance. (Meanwhile, with some success, Carrà had also attempted to paint a picture of action and violence. His subject was the funeral

71. *What the Tram Said to Me,* by Carlo Carrà

72. *Dancer in Blue,* by Gino Severini

of the anarchist Galli, an event that had taken place in 1904.)

When these pictures were finally exhibited, the reaction was hardly what the artists had hoped for. The Italian painter and critic Ardengo Soffici (1879–1964) wrote an article for *La Voce,* published in Florence, in which he took the exhibitors to task for their ignorance of contemporary developments. Severini returned from Paris and was equally horrified at their backwardness. Boccioni and Soffici fell into a fistfight; and since Soffici immediately afterward took up the futurist cause, someone clearly must have proved a point.

Severini's criticisms could not be so readily dismissed, and Boccioni, Carrà, and Marinetti soon made a hasty trip to Paris to catch up on the latest works at the Salon d'Automne. The trip was a fruitful one. Upon his return, Boccioni drastically altered a series of paintings he had already begun. These were called *States of Mind* (I, "The Farewells"; II, "Those Who Go"; III, "Those Who Stay"). In them, a new and more complicated cubist conception of space was combined with the emotional expression of states of mind—for Parisian painters were not interested in states of mind. The mood of *States of Mind II* (Plate 70) is established by sweeping diagonal planes, repeated forms, and overall bluish tones. The effect is of people moving quickly away, and the spectator becomes involved and senses their hurried departures and numb sadness. This sort of emotional effect is at odds with the cool formal arrangements of analytical cubism.

Carrà also produced a painting in which contemporary life is expressed through a modern style—*What the Tram Said to Me* (Plate 71). Here all the noise and bustle of a crowded city street is brought to life through jagged forms, flashing light, and shifting shadows.

These arresting works created a sensation when exhibited in Paris in February, 1912. Marinetti publicized them in his typical aggressive fashion and increased the uproar. The champion of cubism, Apollinaire, took great pride in sensitivity to changing artistic winds. Accordingly, he had to begrudge the futurists some praise for their concern with modern life, its vitality and movement. The exhibition then toured Europe for a year. Futurism had arrived as an international style; but like many modern styles, its initial phase was to last only until the eve of World War I.

Between 1912 and 1914, the futurist artists independently expanded their personal styles. Only the magazine *Lacerba,* which was committed to the cause of futurism, continued to recognize a common bond between their styles. Severini, for example, had always been closer to Parisian trends. His *Dancer in Blue* (Plate 72) is basically a cubist painting put into motion. The bright color and the forms suggested by curves, rather than angles, differ somewhat from analytical cubist works. The trick of pasting sequins on the canvas, however, is borrowed directly from them.

Severini was intrigued by nightlife as a futurist subject, as can be seen in his ambitious *Dynamic Hieroglyph of the Bal Tabarin* (Plate 73). By "dynamic hieroglyph," Severini meant that it was a dynamic (in this sense, futurist) visual synthesis of the rhythms of the Paris café as he remembered them later in Italy.

"Synthesis" is a vague word encountered with dismaying frequency in the literature

73. *Dynamic Hieroglyph of the Bal Tabarin,* by Gino Severini

74. *Little Girl Running on the Balcony,* by Giacomo Balla

In the case of Severini's dynamic hieroglyph, the lines and forms are freely associated with the subject matter and do not specifically describe individual objects. The dancers' ruffles flounce across the picture; there are disembodied faces and a man in evening dress, giddy pennants, and the words "Bowling," "Polka," and "Valse" (waltz). Through the fragmentation, we feel the gaiety of the scene.

Balla remained in Rome to develop his own style of futurism, founded on a divisionist theory of color. Series of simultaneous photographs of figures in motion had deeply impressed him. *Little Girl Running on the Balcony* (Plate 74) shows how he synthesized these photographic effects and divisionist spots of color. In the publication of the collected futurist manifestoes in 1914, a short paragraph was added by Marinetti: "Outside the atmosphere in which we live are only shadows. We futurists ascend towards the highest and most radiant peak and proclaim ourselves Lords of Light, for already we drink from the live founts of the sun." With *Mercury Passing before the Sun as Seen through a Telescope* (Plate 75), Balla abstractly passed beyond the earthly rush of the motor car into these "live founts of the sun," as Marinetti had proposed.

Along with his sculptural experimentation, Boccioni extended his theories of dynamism and painted the explosive *Dynamism of a Cyclist* (Plate 76). This picture is almost a pure abstract and resembles somewhat the works of Kandinsky, a pioneer in modern art whom we shall study shortly. Boccioni, ironically, was killed in a riding accident in 1916 while on leave to recover from war wounds.

The futurists had idealized war as "the only health-giver in the world"; hence such pictures as Severini's *The Charge* and Carrà's *Pursuit* (Plates 77, 78). The ran-

pertaining to art. Artists themselves have a peculiar affection for it. In ancient Greek, synthesis means "putting together"; since this is the original and simplest definition, it would seem wiser and less confusing to memorize it and go no further, thereby avoiding the many unnecessarily ambiguous uses of the word. "Fragmentation" is another word to cope with. When we read that a picture is fragmented or that an artist employs the technique of fragmentation, we might simply think of it in this way: if someone were to shatter a plate on which a scene or a figure had been painted, he might then gather the bits and pieces on a table and try to reassemble them. Until he succeeded, the original painted design would be "fragmented." In other words, in artistic usage, "fragmentation" is a deliberate *dis*assembling and rearranging.

dom letters at the left in *Pursuit* commemorate a French victory by Marshal Joffre. The patriotism of the futurists was unbridled, as can be seen in Carrà's abstract creation *Patriotic Celebration* (Plate 79). The slogan "VI(II)VA(AA) IL RE(EE)" ("Long live the king!") spins wildly around the center, as the sounds of motors ("TRRRR, BRRRR, traak tatatraak") rumble and bounce about the edges. Names of various newspapers and journals, such as the futurist *Lacerba,* and words alluding to modern urban life and entertainment ("street," "noises," "sports," "music,"

75. *Mercury Passing before the Sun as Seen through a Telescope,* by Giacomo Balla

76. *Dynamism of a Cyclist,* by Umberto Boccioni

77. *The Charge,* by Gino Severini

78. *Pursuit,* by Carlo Carrà

79. *Patriotic Celebration,* by Carlo Carrà

"songs") are scattered across the surface. The title of the work is perhaps reflected in the repetition of "Italy" and "Italian" at several spots throughout the canvas.

Because of pictures like these, the world began henceforth to associate modern art with revolution and violence. Ironically, the war that so thrilled the futurists brought an end to their ideals, for afterward the survivors went on to paint in another style.

Die Brücke and the Viennese School

IN 1905 a circle of restless young German artists founded a revolutionary group called Die Brücke ("The Bridge"). Led by Ernst Ludwig Kirchner (1880–1938), this group included Erich Heckel (1883–   ), Karl Schmidt-Rottluff (1884–   ), and Fritz Bleyl (1880–   ). They were all architectural students, and only Kirchner had received any formal art training. They detested the cruel social caste system of Germany, especially the way in which the lower classes were suppressed both economically and educationally; yet they had no sympathy for ignorance. Their motto was "Odi profanum vulgus" ("I hate the uninitiated common masses"), and they denounced the stodgy "Victorian" German society for permitting conditions to continue as they were. German expressionism was born of this crying need for change.

Die Brücke believed fanatically in the constructive joys and ideas of group activity. Everything should be accomplished together, with mutual enthusiasm. The only drawback to this theory was that, while sounding the signal to plunge ahead, it left little time for individual reflection, logic, or order.

Together the members of the group took over a former cobbler's workshop in a working-class district of Dresden. Together they built furniture, carved stools, and put canvases around the walls of the group's new home and studio. Together they began to take drawing lessons from Fritz Schumacher (1869–1957), a distinguished town planner and architect who taught at the Dresden Academy of Art. Schumacher had impressed on them the need for unity and for personal expression. Among outsiders, he alone suspected the true quality of the group. "In my horror at the messy drawings of those students," he remembered much later, "I could not pretend to understand the young ducklings who swam away from me, unexperienced mother hen that I was. But if I remained doubtful for the time being about the artistic value, I had on the other hand a definite feeling for the human value."

The group insisted that "art depends on inspiration, not on technique." Meanwhile, Sigmund Freud's radical ideas on psychoanalysis and the subconscious were being published; and in music Arnold Schönberg's revolutionary scale system defied and openly broke with the harmonic laws of the past. The old conservative, safe and orderly life was starting to crumble. Die Brücke looked for inspiration in everything not associated with academic culture. Kirchner reintroduced the woodcut, with its primitive strength and energy, from its native southern Germany. Heckel revived wood carvings, and Kirchner colored them. Schmidt-Rottluff made the first lithographs directly on stone. Together the group "discovered" African Negro art and idolized Van Gogh, Gauguin, and Munch.

It should be remembered that Die Brücke's development came at more or less the same time as that of the Fauves; yet the sources from which they drew inspiration clearly distinguished them from the Fauves. The violent, anguished use of color by Van Gogh and Gauguin was extremely personal and at times exotic. Some of the "primitive" elements in their art could indeed be found in the work of Derain, Vlaminck, and Picasso; nevertheless, it would seem that the Germans arrived at their bold style independently. Die Brücke had also been influenced by their studies of native art from Africa and the South Pacific in the Dresden Museum of Ethnography. They also learned much about the use of symbolic color from Signac and were moved by the sorrow and melancholy of Munch's paintings.

It must be emphasized that, though their art had vague links with Africa and the South Seas, these young artists were thoroughly German or "Northern" in outlook. The barbaric savagery of some of their paintings may disguise a basic severity and starkness that harks back to the age of the Teutonic barbarians. Northern artists and writers have frequently explored dark and neurotic themes of decadence and torment. Their preoccupation has been with the troubled human condition. Such Northern attitudes, therefore, should be expected to show themselves in the expressionism of Die Brücke. Furthermore, working together in this communal spirit was thought to be a Northern idea, with roots in the medieval guild system.

Like the futurists, the Brücke group vigorously rejected all academic conventions. Cubism was an art of calm analysis; Die Brücke's was one of highly imaginative personal and emotional expression. Above anyone or anything else, Van Gogh had the greatest single influence on the German group's ideas.

Kirchner's intellectual ability and his preoccupation with theory automatically made him the group's leader. His *Self-portrait with a Model* (Plate 80) sets the style of their work. The viewer is immediately struck by the violently contrasting primary colors, the bold play of horizontal stripes and flat patterns, the masklike faces, and the dominating character of the artist. Color is used expressively rather than to define

80. *Self-portrait with a Model,* by Ernst Ludwig Kirchner

space or model the forms. Kirchner's *Two Dancers* (Plate 81) goes a step further in its angular distortions and blaring colors. The faces and figures are more grotesque than in the self-portrait; they are influenced both by Gothic woodcuts and by Picasso's African-inspired heads. Kirchner never painted abstract compositions, because his emotional involvement with reality was too great.

The Brücke artists worked in Dresden during the winter and by the North Sea in the summer. It was there, by the sea, that they began painting boldly simplified landscapes in bright colors. Schmidt-Rottluff, in his *Forest* (Plate 82), created artificial but vibrant arrangements of red and blue tree trunks singing out against green, orange, and blue. He followed Gauguin's method

81. *Two Dancers,* by Ernst Ludwig Kirchner

82. *Forest,* by Karl Schmidt-Rottluff

of using unnatural and imaginative color. Between 1907 and 1913, Schmidt-Rottluff painted landscapes regularly every summer, such as the *View of Lofthus* (Plate 83).

Heckel's particular enthusiasms were for "the visions of Van Gogh and Munch"; he also admired primitive art. A synthesis of these two interests can be seen in such paintings as *Two Men Seated at a Table* (Plate 84). We are presented with an extremely sinister, even frightening scene. The faces are again masklike in a primitive manner, but are highly expressive. One wonders what terrible thing is about to take place. Is the man on the right about to sit, or is he rising to knife the other? Have others just left them to themselves, or are the empty chairs for new arrivals? The agonized image of Christ on the wall heightens the morbid atmosphere; the portrait of a man with downcast eyes on another wall of the room seems to understand the secret but will tell us nothing.

84. *Two Men Seated at a Table,* by Erich Heckel

83. *View of Lofthus,* by Karl Schmidt-Rottluff

85. *Children in a Wood,* by Otto Müller

86. *Garden with Red and Yellow Roses,* by Emil Nolde

In 1910 Otto Müller (1874–1930) joined the Brücke group. For Müller, who was a descendant of gypsies, pictures of innocent figures set in dreamlike landscapes were an obsession. As a reaction against the modern mechanized world, he created a never-never land of gypsies and naked children in natural surroundings (Plate 85). This sort of idyllic world was like that which Gauguin had brought to life in his Tahitian canvases. Müller's sadly nostalgic images stand somewhat apart from the torment of the rest of the Brücke group, but his elfin figures remain expressive symbols of his contempt for "civilized" cities, a contempt shared by all the Brücke members.

In 1906 the group persuaded Emil Nolde (1867–1956) to join them, but he was to remain a member for only fifteen months. Nolde always stood somewhat outside the group. He had been painting longer than the others and had developed his own private vision. Though his style was similar to that of the Brücke artists, he remained "the great solitary of German expressionism." Earlier in his career he had painted naturalistically, but with a Northern sense of strange grimness. In 1905 he abruptly changed his style after being introduced to the paintings of Van Gogh. This influence can be seen in a series of garden paintings executed in 1907–1908 (Plate 86). His interest in primitive art was extended by a trip to the Pacific islands in 1913–1914. He quickly adopted the "stylized, rhythmical and decorative" qualities of Pacific native art in his own work. Probably more clearly than any other painter who was influenced by primitive art, Nolde was able to answer the question "Why is it that we artists are so entranced by the primitive expression of the savages? . . . With the material in his hand, between his fingers, the artist creates his work. The expressed purpose is desire for and love of creation. The absolute originality, the intense, frequently grotesque expression of strength and life in the simplest form—that could be the factor which gives us so much joy."

In Nolde's *Dancers* (Plate 87), we see him applying this primitive "expression of strength and life in the simplest form" to his own art. The beautiful, strong colors are handled masterfully. Nolde felt deeply about color, and he might have been speaking for all fellow artists who have been emotionally moved by color when, most poetically, he expressed his feelings this way: "Colors, the materials of the painter; colors in their own lives, weeping and laughing, dream and bliss, hot and sacred, like love songs . . . like songs and glorious chorales! Colors in vibration, pealing like silver bells and clanging like bronze bells, proclaiming happiness, passion and love, soul, blood and death."

The Brücke group moved to Berlin in 1910. This move marked the beginning of the gradual breakup of the group. Later, in 1913, Kirchner wrote a history of the association, which the other members considered a highly displeasing distortion of the facts. This unfortunate incident caused the final disintegration of the once inseparable artistic circle.

The feeling of unrest that drove the artists to new ideas in Dresden, Paris, and Milan was evident also in Vienna, but in a slightly different way. "Jugendstil," the German variant of Art Nouveau, had been so called after the magazine *Jugend* ("Youth"), first published in 1896. The style, in which a sinuous and decorative line was the essential element, was practically interchangeable with its French and English counterparts.

87. *Dancers,* by Emil Nolde

The Brücke group washed their hands of it in contempt. In Vienna, however, two important painters, Egon Schiele (1890–1918) and Oskar Kokoschka (1886–   ), gave a last twist to Jugendstil. In contrast to the angular harshness of the Brücke painters, Schiele developed a lovely manner in which he put coiling line through the most dramatic contortions. Schiele's paintings are brightly colored and intricately patterned, and his drawing is superb, as is seen in the *Portrait of Edith, the Artist's Wife* (Plate 88).

Some authorities claim that Kokoschka's style derived from the decorative tendencies of Jugendstil. There may be some truth in this, but Kokoschka himself has said that the strongest influence during his youth was

89. *Portrait of Professor Auguste Farel,* by Oskar Kokoschka

Austrian baroque art, particularly the elaborate ceiling and wall paintings in the churches of that period. In 1904, at the age of eighteen, Kokoschka entered the Vienna School of Arts and Crafts; and in 1908 he held his first exhibition as a painter. His creative energy was too great to channel into just one area of artistic activity; he also wrote plays, illustrated books, sculpted, and designed posters and decorative panels. Outstanding among his early works are a series of portraits done in 1909–1910. These are penetrating and dramatic character studies. What made them expressionistic was Kokoschka's feverish search for the soul of his subject and the exaggerated linear style he used in achieving this. A fine example of these expressionistic studies is the *Portrait of Professor Auguste Farel* (Plate 89); the sitter was a famous zoologist who lived in Switzerland. The subdued color is relatively unimportant, for it is the expressionistic drawing of the face and hands that commands our attention.

Kokoschka's talent was recognized by Herwarth Walden (1878–   ), the writer, gallery owner, and publisher of the influential magazine *Der Sturm* and the Viennese artist was encouraged to move to Berlin in 1910. From then onward, he played an important role in the development of German expressionism. Kokoschka's style grew much freer in its drawing and in the use of thicker, brighter pigments in later works such as *The Heathen* (Plate 90). He remained a dominant figure in European painting for decades, much admired for his personal and imaginative transformation of reality.

88. *Portrait of Edith, the Artist's Wife,* by Egon Schiele

90. *The Heathen,* by Oskar Kokoschka

Development of Abstract Art: Blaue Reiter and De Stijl

THE TYPICAL CONTEMPORARY lack of concern with natural appearances in art is due entirely to the experiments of such artists as Kupka, Delaunay, Kandinsky, Mondrian, and Malevich. These pioneers of abstract painting stressed the relationship between abstract art and music, for they considered both as pure art forms. They began to think of art as, fundamentally, the arrangement of lines, shapes, and colors on a flat surface. These arrangements were intended to give pleasure through their own harmonies, and reference to the outside world or identifiable subject matter was no longer necessary.

Before these new trends emerged, the impressionists had developed an almost perfect technique for representing the natural world. Photography, which was rapidly gaining in use, now offered the ultimate in accuracy for recording outward appearances. In reaction, artists turned inward to their private worlds. Some, like Kandinsky in his earliest phase, turned to a free development of color in which natural objects were gradually dissolved in a mysterious world of expressive paint. Others such as Mondrian and Malevich evolved a world of pure geometry from their earlier experiments with cubism. Kandinsky eventually followed them into this last particular world of pure abstraction, where emotion is aroused by severe arrangements of basic forms and manipulation of color. Yet there continued the long-standing opposition between the intellectual and the emotional approaches to art, as will be seen below.

At the beginning of the twentieth cen-tury, Munich provided a healthy artistic climate in which to experiment. The dominant style was still Jugendstil, but the Munich artists were conscious of developments in Paris and elsewhere. The arrival of Wassily Kandinsky (1866–1944), a Russian, was to prove extremely important for Munich's artistic life. Kandinsky came to art late, at the age of thirty. His earliest ambition was to become a musician—which is interesting in that, later, he so frequently associated painting with music. Initially, Kandinsky had entered Moscow University in 1886 to study law and economics. There he first came into contact with the rich, unearthly glow of traditional Russian art and medieval icons (holy images); these works made a profound impression on him and greatly influenced his artistic development. Kandinsky also studied Russian folk art and was enchanted by its riotous colors.

In 1895, two years after receiving his law degree, Kandinsky was exposed for the first time to the paintings of the French impressionists. Immediately his mind was made up; he gave up his legal career and took off for Munich, where he enrolled at the Royal Academy. After three years of classes, he began to work independently. Between 1903 and 1908 he traveled widely in France, Tunisia, and Italy, but kept in close touch with developments in Paris all the while. Later he wrote, "Matisse—color. Picasso—form. Two great signposts pointing towards a great end."

Kandinsky's early art, though colorful and free, was not really very close to Fauvism. At first his art had been more influenced by his Russian background, a tendency that was not surprising in the grandson of an Asiatic princess. He became increasingly obsessed with this mysterious world of color in which objects seemed to dissolve. It took

91. *Crinolines,* by Vassily Kandinsky

him some time to re-create it in his paintings. Gradually he turned away from the copying of actual appearances, saying, "I sometimes paint a landscape from memory better than after nature." For a while he painted historical pictures, with the color laid on in flat patches like a decorative tapestry. *Crinolines* (Plate 91), for example, with its flattened figures in historical costume, reminds us that Kandinsky wished to create an art of the imagination. The rough brushwork, however, was boldly modern in spirit.

The Blue Mountain (Plate 92) is another fascinating mixture of the decorative, the Russian fairytale, and the profound. The figures are similar to peasant gingerbread

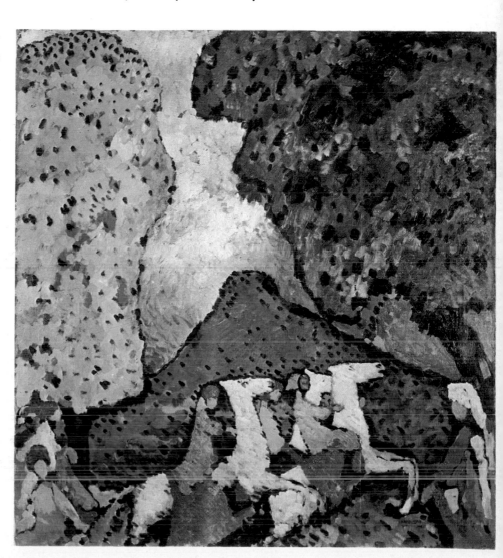

92. *The Blue Mountain,* by Vassily Kandinsky

93. *Paradise,* by Vassily Kandinsky

molds, but the style is divisionist. This painting also shows Kandinsky's awareness of developments in Dresden, in particular of the Brücke group. His concern with the "mystery" of painting gradually led him away from using recognizable figures and objects; but, he asked himself, "What should replace the missing object?" He was afraid of falling into a style in which the final effect would be no more than decorative or ornamental. Consequently, he dedicated himself to the idea of "inner necessity," feeling that "as musical sound acts directly on the soul, so do form and color." The major step between reference to visual reality and the creation of an image completely independent of reality can be seen in *Paradise* and *With the Black Arch* (Plates 93, 94). In the first-mentioned picture, houses and land- scape can still be identified amid the flurry of brushstrokes; in the second, the visionary effect of a landscape as if in motion is made without naturalistic features. Its logic is its own "inner necessity." Through its mysterious colorful world Kandinsky at- tempts to approach a universal truth—a central being at the heart of all things. He felt he would be unable to express this by traditional methods of painting. "To spell out the mysterious through the mysteri- ous—is that not content?" he wrote in 1910. In essence, Kandinsky had created abstract art.

Kandinsky was a skillful organizer as well as a great spiritual and theoretical force. In 1909 he had founded the New Artists' Association in Munich, which by 1911 had already begun to affect the cultural life of

94. *With the Black Arch,* by Vassily Kandinsky

the city. At this time, however, the association split in two. The backward-looking artists considered Kandinsky's new theories of abstract art too dangerous in their implications; a quarrel arose over the exhibition of one of his paintings. Kandinsky, with a few friends, including the young Franz Marc (1880–1916), withdrew from the group. Around Maria Marc's tea table, they created a new group—the Blaue Reiter (its name being taken from one of Kandinsky's pictures, *The Blue Rider*), which was also to be the name of the art magazine they planned to publish.

This progressive group opened an exhibit of its own in the same gallery a few weeks afterward. The artists represented were Kandinsky and Marc, Gabriele Münter (1877–1962), August Macke (1887–1914), Heinrich Campendonk (1889–1957), the two Russians David (1882–1967) and Vladimir (18 –19) Burliuk, and the avant-garde composer Arnold Schönberg (1874–1951), who was also a painter. Kandinsky included two French painters whom he considered important as examples of opposite extremes: Robert Delaunay and Henri Rousseau. By 1912 the Russian Alexei von Jawlensky (1867–1941), as well as Alfred Kubin (1877–1959) and the Swiss Paul Klee (1879–1940), had also joined the Blaue Reiter circle. Touring exhibitions that were arranged by the group showed examples of the various abstract tendencies of the times.

August Macke, though equally involved with the Blaue Reiter group, developed along different lines. Concerning himself very much with color, he was also impressed by cubist simplification and the art of Rousseau. Though interested in representing states of mind and abstract theories, Macke never painted wholly abstract pic-

tures. Influenced by a simple type of cubism, he created doll-like figures that exist in an airless world of their own (Plate 95). Macke, too, was killed early in World War I.

Alexei von Jawlensky was an army officer before he went to study art in Munich. Between 1902 and 1910, he traveled widely and was much affected by the paintings of Matisse and the Fauves that he encountered. Before the outbreak of the war he produced a series of large, powerfully colored heads and simplified figures. *The White Plume* (Plate 97) shows how he was developing toward this style; the figure fills the picture area, and the paint is thick and colorful. In later paintings, his outlines became deliberately more crude and primitive. Although he never became completely an abstract artist, he shared a spiritual bond with his Munich associates. His freely painted works, which owe much to the example of Gauguin and Matisse, remain expressive and symbolic images (Plate 96).

Germany, and in particular Munich, had been the natural place to study for many Russian artists. They did not, however, neglect Paris. From 1906 onward, Diaghilev's Russian ballet company and its designers created an enormous stir in Paris. Serge Diaghilev (1872–1929) conceived a ballet in which music, dancing, décor (set decoration), and costumes all formed a single brilliantly unified whole. Soloists, no matter how distinguished, formed part of that unity, as did every member of the chorus. In décor and costumes he also broke new ground by commissioning designs from well-known artists. In the past, ballet décor had all too frequently been limited to a misty, vaguely romantic backdrop containing a forest or a lake. Through such commissions a new integration of costumes and settings was achieved. Some art

95. *Separation,* by August Macke

movements such as rayonism, developed by Larionov and Gontcharova, found their fullest expression in the theater. Between 1911 and 1914, Mikhail Larionov (1881–1964) and his wife Natalia Gontcharova (1881–1962), Russian artists who exhibited at the second Blaue Reiter show in 1912, launched a style to which they gave the dismaying name "rayonism." Influenced by cubism and futurism, this style was characterized by luminous rays that its creators called "lines of force" (Plates 98, 99).

Later, Diaghilev was forced to turn more and more to Western Europe for inspiration. As always, he sought the finest artists, so that eventually Picasso, Matisse, Gris, Braque, Derain, Rouault, and others were all enlisted to contribute their creative genius to his Ballet Russe productions.

Another significant Russian painter, Kazimir Malevich (1878–1935), founded a new movement that he called "suprematism." Malevich had run through a whole gamut of Western European styles, ending with cubism, but none seemed to suit him for long. Disenchanted, he proceeded to create a completely abstract art based on the simplest geometric forms. His first suprematist picture was a black square on a white background. Nothing could be simpler. The two contrasting colors he considered the basis of all art, and he felt that "reality in art was the sensational effect of color itself." His position was later explained by members of a progressive school called the Bauhaus:

The representation of an object, in itself . . . is something that has nothing to do with art, although the use of representation in a work of art does not rule out the possibility of its

96. *Still Life,* by Alexeivon Jawlensky

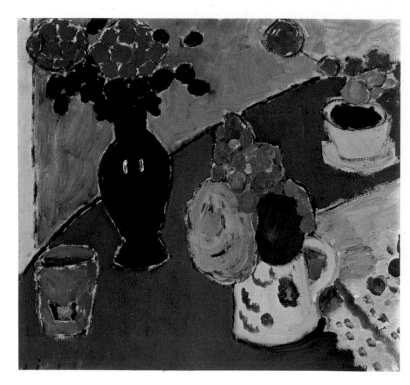

97. *The White Plume,*
by Alexei von Jawlensky

being of a high artistic order. For the suprematist, therefore, the proper means is the one that provides the fullest expression of pure feeling and ignores the habitually accepted object. The object in itself is meaningless to him; and the ideas of the conscious mind are worthless. Feeling is the decisive factor . . . and *thus art arrives at non-objective representation*—at suprematism.

Eight Red Rectangles (Plate 100), for example, presents its own language of form. Malevich expected that his pure art form should, like music, be understood without reference to the world of appearances. The development of this abstract style was important in Russia and elsewhere for its new approach to basic design principles in the applied arts and architecture.

Painters in Holland who were aware of contemporary developments in France started the group known as De Stijl ("The Style"). Holland produced an equally spare and harmonious art based on the same fundamentals that Malevich had applied in evolving suprematism in Russia. The De Stijl group was made up of artists and designers whose achievements soon affected both modern architecture and interior design. The revolution they caused in typography (the art of printing with type, which involves design of lettering styles, or typefaces, and effective page layouts) and advertising layout is still apparent today. Its Dutch origins very likely gave this new art form its logic, simplicity, and severe, orderly structure. Fancy brushwork or extravagant personal mannerisms were not to be tolerated.

Piet Mondrian (1872–1944), De Stijl's greatest genius, remained true to his own early artistic concepts during the whole of his career. Having begun to draw and paint while very young in his village home, he left his teaching studies in order to begin

98. *Vase with Rayonist Flowers,* by Natalia Gontcharova

99. *Rayonist Interior,* by Mikhail Larionov

100. *Eight Red Rectangles,*
by Kazimir Malevich

formal art training in Amsterdam. He painted in a rather impressionist manner until 1911, when he went to Paris. There he quickly became an admirer of the cubist paintings of Picasso and Léger.

The important early phase of his career occurred between 1911 and 1916, when he sought to abstract the basic lines and harmonies of trees, still lifes, and seascapes. The recognizable abstracted forms became simpler and simpler, much as they had in the paintings of Kandinsky; but there was a major difference. Kandinsky had sought

in nature the mystery and suggestion of color. Mondrian was searching for the underlying lines of balance in nature. At first glance, *Composition in Line and Color* (Plate 101), dating from 1912–1913, suggests a cubist still life, but the objects have been turned into a series of vertical and horizontal lines broken by an occasional arc. The color range of yellow ochers and grays is typically cubist.

When World War I broke out in 1914, Mondrian was in Holland, which remained a neutral country. Unable to return to Paris,

101. *Composition in Line and Color,*
by Piet Mondrian

102. *Geometric Composition,* by Theo van Doesburg

he spent his time on a series of pictures based on the sea waves and breakwaters at Domburg (Plate 103). Because of their crisscrossed and short horizontal lines, these have been called Mondrian's "plus-minus" works. The rhythm of the waves rolling into shore is expressed by short horizontal strokes that gradually spread toward the bottom of the picture. Though this is an abstract picture, Mondrian was dissatisfied with even such minimal reference to natural effects. "The emotion of beauty is always obstructed by the appearance of the 'object'; therefore the object must be eliminated from the picture."

Mondrian had reached this important conclusion in 1915, the momentous year when he met Theo van Doesburg (1883–1931), (Plate 102) the nervously brilliant critic, painter, architect, and poet. The following year he became acquainted with Bart van der Leck (1876–1958), who had produced abstract pictures composed of simple rectangles in black and the primary colors of

103. *Composition No. 10: Breakwater and Sea,* by Piet Mondrian

104. *Geometric Composition II*
by Bart van der Leck

red, yellow, and blue (Plate 104). Van Doesburg had been creating geometric abstracts as well. Upon seeing that their work was similar, the three artists decided to join forces. Along with the architects Oud, Wils, Van't Hoff, and Rietveld and the sculptor Georges Vantongerloo (1886–), they founded the group De Stijl and the magazine.

Mondrian followed Van der Leck's example and introduced the simple red, yellow, and blue rectangles into his own work. This made it possible for him to create an art with none of the despised reference to natural appearances. As a further refinement, in about 1920 Mondrian began to separate his rectangles with strong black vertical and horizontal bars (Plate 105). He explained that "the pictorial space became white, black or gray: the form became red, blue or yellow." Eventually his pictures were composed in the simplest way: the verticals contained primary colors, and the horizontals the "noncolors" (black, white, and gray). This balance of contrasts he named "neoplasticism."

Neoplasticism was to find its most logical outlet of expression in the architecture of De Stijl. The architectual style was basically a severe arrangement of cubes, with primary colors applied for contrast. The new architecture produced examples both in Holland and abroad and influenced such great contemporary architects as Le Corbusier, Gropius, and Mies van der Rohe.

105. *Composition with Red, Yellow, and Blue,* by Piet Mondrian

The "Peintres Maudits"

THE COLORFUL bohemian way of life in Paris is legendary. But after the turn of the century its carefree surface could not always disguise an increasingly sinister undercurrent of degradation and vice. Too frequently, drink and drugs went hand in hand with desperation and self-destruction. In France, an artist who loses control of his life, dissipates his talent, or ends in final misery is known as a *peintre maudit,* an "accursed" or "doomed painter." Four such men were Amedeo Modigliani (1884–1920), Chaim Soutine (1894–1943), Jules Pascin (1885–1930), and Maurice Utrillo (1883–1955).

In their homelessness, intensity, and the passionate involvement of their lives, they seemed to be haunted—even hunted. In 1906, Modigliani left his native Italy for Paris, where a combination of drinking, drug addiction, and reckless living was to kill him at the age of thirty-six. He was incredibly handsome, both shy and quarrelsome, yet capable of great charm and of dominating conversation. He was usually dressed respectably and cleanly, in contrast to most of the other aspiring young Parisian artists. (Picasso himself started a fashion by wearing a "monkey suit," a denim coverall, with a workman's cap while painting all night and a soft felt hat from Spain for "dressing up." Furthermore, after examining some American Civil War photographs at Gertrude Stein's, Picasso decided that he looked like Lincoln and changed his hair style in the hope that the resemblance might become even more noticeable.)

Modigliani was known to the artists who gathered around Picasso—it may have been at the suggestion of Picasso that he moved to Montmartre—but he was not one of them. In his early days in Paris he led a rather solitary life; nevertheless, he was as clear in his ambition to become an artist, in particular a sculptor, as any of them. His restless temperament had led him to Paris, where he could find the chaotic milieu in which it was necessary for him to live. Despite his increasing addiction to cheap wine and drugs, "Modi's" work got better and better. His chief interest continued to be sculpture. His drawings were mainly sketches for sculpture, and at night he would go out with a wheelbarrow to steal stone from building sites.

Modigliani found two art dealers and soon was no longer an unknown. He continued to draw feverishly, and out of his experiments his distinctive style began to emerge. Never without a sketch pad and pencil, he constantly made jottings of what he saw about him. And these were almost always of people: the human form was the main subject of his art. Portraits and nudes dominated his output. The fact that his painting depended heavily on drawing does not mean that Modigliani did not understand the qualities of paint; on the contrary, he made full use of painting techniques. The overall texture of his paintings is extremely varied, perfectly calculated and perfectly achieved. He always used a limited range of color and tones in his paintings. The quietly melancholy *Woman with a Tie* (Plate 106) is typical in this way. The subdued flesh tones and dominant greenish grays are brightened only by the sudden red touch of the mouth.

Modigliani's sculpture, too, shows him to be a master of textural effects. There has always been some difficulty in determining how many sculptures he created from 1912 on, and to what years they belong.

106. *Woman with a Tie*, by Amedeo Modigliani

It is certain that this date marked a brilliant change in his view of art and launched not only a new development in his own career but also in the whole course of European sculpture. His new constructions clearly testified that Modigliani had looked long and carefully at the art of the African primitive masters who were the current enthusiasm of the Paris avant-garde. But his works were in no sense copies, for each of them bears the genuine feeling of Modigliani's vivid personality. The lines of his sculpture have the same clean, precise qualities that are typical of his painting and draftsmanship (Plates 107, 108).

It was not until this sculptural phase that Modigliani reached full maturity as a painter. Unlike so many of his contemporaries, he remained a basically representational painter, exploring the problems of portraiture and nude studies with great success. But Modigliani's way of life was so wildly undisciplined, and had been for so long, that he was unable to fight off the tuberculosis which killed him in 1920. He died in dreadful poverty.

Chaim Soutine, like Modigliani, showed all the signs of restless torment in his painting as in his life. Whereas Modigliani's canvases give the impression that he was able to achieve a temporary spiritual repose in his art, however, the paintings of Soutine reflect the tortured violence of his life. He painted with an almost insane ferocity. He once finished a picture and found afterward that, in painting it, he had seriously dislocated his thumb. The energy and concentration he brought to the creative act was so great that he was not aware of the mishap at the time.

Soutine came from a miserably poor Lithuanian Jewish family. The Jewish religious code of his boyhood was so strict that

107. *Head,* by Amedeo Modigliani

108. *Man with a Glass of Wine,* by Amedeo Modigliani

he was forbidden to draw or create any image whatsoever; but Soutine's passion to become an artist could not be suppressed. He stole crayons when he was seven and drew whenever he could. Having been expelled from school, he set out to study painting—first at Minsk, then at the School of Fine Arts in Vilna, and at last in Paris, where he arrived in 1913. But the École des Beaux-Arts was suited neither to Soutine's temperament nor to his strong ideas about painting. Soon he found a more sympathetic atmosphere in La Ruche ("The Beehive"), a studio block where Modigliani, Léger, and the Russian Jewish painter Marc Chagall (1887–) all lived. Modigliani, who was kind, sensitive, and always alert to other talents, introduced Soutine to his dealer Zborowski. Through this contact, Soutine was able to sell his first few paintings.

The paintings that Soutine did at La Ruche, though not yet formed in his mature manner, already have the terrifying emotional intensity that marks his style. These included a series of gladioli paintings of enormous power and some remarkable views of Montmartre. In his depiction of reality, Soutine distorted his forms with wild and rhythmic effect. This was carried almost to extremes in his important period at Céret, where, in his most productive phase (1920–1922), he finished over two hundred paintings. In their violent upheavals these remind one of nothing so much as earthquakes.

Soutine always painted directly from nature. This could cause practical difficulties, such as happened during the period when he was depicting slabs of butchered meat. At La Ruche, he had made friends with the employees of a local slaughterhouse and practiced painting pieces of beef that he got from them. In 1922 he painted an admira-

ble *Side of Beef.* In 1925 he got his hands on the entire carcass of a steer and managed to get it up into his studio, where he worked at painting it for days on end. When the carcass got too dry in the heat, buckets of blood were brought from the slaughterhouse to pour over it. The paintings are full of rich, bloody colors. But not surprisingly, his neighbors complained loudly of the smell.

After the beef episode, Soutine did a number of pictures of plucked or half-plucked fowl (Plate 109). These are still life, but, more importantly, still life of flesh. Also at this time, Soutine was doing a series of portraits of youths in the uniforms of their work—pastry cooks, bellboys, and the

109. *Dead Fowl,* by Chaim Soutine

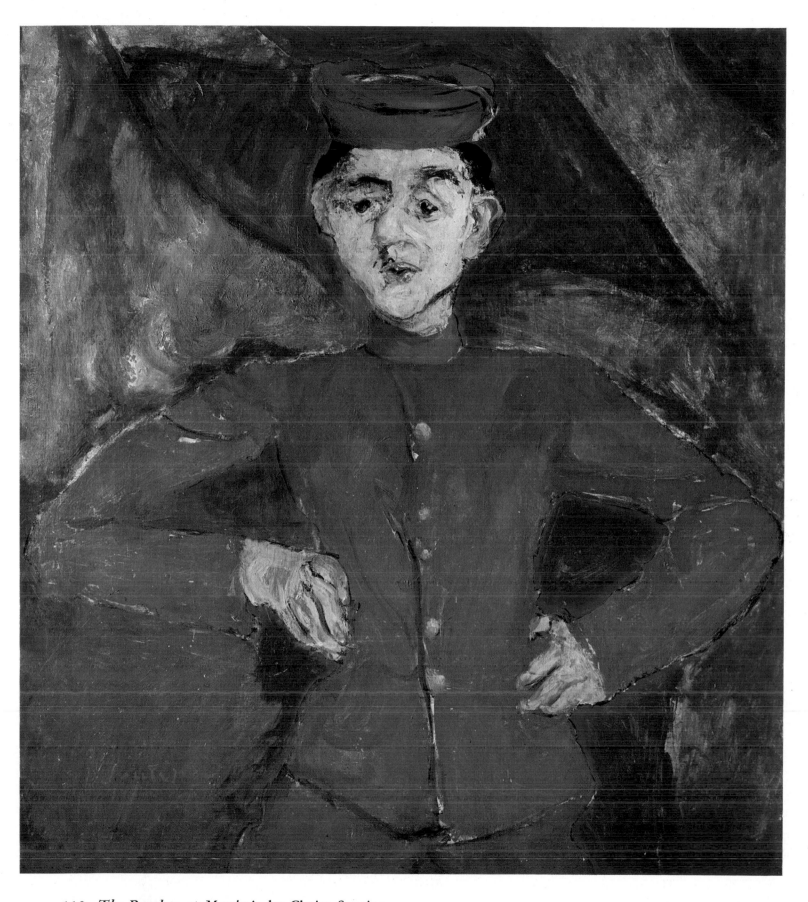

110. *The Pageboy at Maxim's,* by Chaim Soutine

like (Plate 110). Alone among Soutine's paintings in their charm and sentiment, these seem to have pleased everyone.

Soutine went on painting through the 1930's. His last great series was of tree-filled landscapes in which he seemed to return in spirit to the woodlands of his native Lithuania. Despite the danger to Jews, Soutine remained in France during World War II, and it was there that he died, before the war's end. It was an entirely appropriate gesture of Picasso to defy the regulations of the German occupation by joining in Soutine's funeral procession.

Jules Pascin, whose real name was Julius Pincas, was another artistic wanderer. A Bulgarian by birth, the son of a Sephardic Jew, he may have studied art in Vienna. It is impossible to say with certainty what his background was, since Pascin liked to cover his tracks and create an air of mystery about where he had come from and what he was doing. As a young man he lived in Munich, where he was well known for the clear, cynical drawings that he contributed to the magazine *Simplicissimus*. By 1905 he had arrived in Paris, and his early work there sometimes resembles that of the Fauves. A few years later a marked cubist tendency appeared in his style. But the artist with whom he had the most in common was Henri de Toulouse-Lautrec. Like Lautrec, Pascin had an interest in painting subjects from the world of low entertainment; like him, also, Pascin worked out a style of rapid sketching in a very fluid oil technique.

During these years he was probably better known in Germany than in France. In 1905 he exhibited at the famous Paul Kassiner Gallery in Berlin, alongside the work of Van Gogh and several others. In 1911 his pictures were shown at the Berlin Sezession

exhibition and were considered to be in the line of German expressionism. In short, just as he had no personal roots, Pascin had no deep permanent artistic roots. When World War I broke out, to avoid being drafted by any European country, Pascin fled to the United States. In New York he had his first one-man show, but his sales were very poor. He decided to go south, traveling at various times to Mexico, Cuba, and New Orleans. On these trips he preferred to use watercolor or chalk-and-pencil overlaid with watercolor washes. These were ideal media for quick impressionistic note-taking.

It was typical of Pascin that he should have returned to Paris almost immediately after he became a naturalized American citizen. He was back in the French capital by 1920, the year Modigliani died. He never met the Italian artist, but he certainly took over from him as leading bohemian of the day. Pascin's work sold well during the 1920's, and he became famous for his lavish parties. During this period, female nudes and semi-nudes were his most usual subjects. More drawn than painted, they emerge in a delicate luminous glow from the shimmering light of the background (Plate 111). They appear casual, but actually many hours of work went into their seemingly spontaneous poses. While still in his early middle age, Pascin committed suicide in 1930.

A painter almost totally lacking in artistic purpose was Maurice Utrillo. It is hardly an exaggeration to say that he often painted pictures only to buy his next drink. When Modigliani first met Utrillo, he was obliged to pick him up off the floor of a bar and march off, carrying with him two bottles of wine. They ended that night, as well as many future ones, in the police station.

Utrillo was born the illegitimate son of

Suzanne Valadon (1867–1938), an acrobat turned artist's model. His mother, who frequently posed for Renoir, had artistic talent herself and was encouraged by her painter friends to develop it. Degas, the greatest draftsman of the age, gave her lessons. It was as a result of her interest in art that Utrillo was first given painting materials. The circumstances were not happy, for the paints were to provide occupational therapy for Utrillo, who was committed to a home for alcoholics at the age of eighteen. After taking some art lessons, he developed a facility for turning out a staggering number of scenes of his native Montmartre, the picturesque artistic colony where he was born and lived. In Utrillo's pictures the interest in humanity and self-expression that characterized the postimpressionist painters is not to be found. His compositions tend to follow a general set pattern. Usually, a broad expanse of road in the foreground recedes into the distance, and buildings close in the composition at both sides (Plate 112).

Utrillo's enormous output of paintings was a direct result of economic necessity, the extravagance of his way of life, and his constant need for drink. Even when he was briefly out of Paris, he painted the squares and streets he knew so well, from memory. He worked quickly to lay down a charcoal sketch on the canvas; next, he would rapidly paint in oils over the sketch, with a spontaneous technique that quite often became simply careless. At his best, however, Utrillo is an artist with pleasing qualities. His feeling for stonework and plastered buildings makes him a master of picturesque city scenes in many works.

111. *Mirelle,* by Jules Pascin

112. *Rue Norvins,* by Maurice Utrillo

113. *Interior with Goldfish,* by Henri Matisse

114. *The Piano Lesson,* by Henri Matisse

AFTER HIS heroic period as leader of the Fauves, Matisse arrived at a much more established position in the art world. By 1908, the cubists had taken over as leaders of the avant-garde. During the winter of 1907–1908 the famous Académie Matisse was organized. These new art classes attracted scores of students from America, Central Europe, and Scandinavia. Matisse taught in the same way that he had been instructed by Gustave Moreau. Like Moreau, Matisse had no wish to force old academic traditions on his students, nor did he encourage them to imitate his own style.

It was at this time that Matisse produced several important works. His qualities as draftsman, designer, and colorist can be seen in six paintings of this period which represent goldfish. In *Interior with Goldfish* (Plate 113), the three principal elements—the bowl of goldfish, the flowers, and the nude figure (which is a painting of one of his own sculptures, the *Reclining Nude* of 1907)—are perfectly balanced against one another. The design they form is not merely flat and ornamental. These juggling contrasts between a flatly colored decorative surface and the lively play of different elements against each other in depth are a characteristic feature of Matisse's style.

Between 1915 and 1918 certain obviously cubist attitudes crept into Matisse's paintings. *The Piano Lesson* (Plate 114) hints strongly at this; but more than any analytic cubist painting, it reorganizes the actual world with an austere, classic beauty and gravity that belongs only to the greatest art.

The *Decorative Figure on an Ornamental Background* (Plate 115), painted in 1927, is

115. *Decorative Figure on an Ornamental Background,* by Henri Matisse

116. *Jeannette IV,* by Henri Matisse

an amazingly brilliant work. Here, more than in any other of his paintings, the decorative and patternmaking aspect of Matisse's style is shown. For some years after this, Matisse turned away from easel paintings and concentrated on drawings, prints, and sculpture; but his best sculptures were probably those he had executed between 1909 and 1913, when he produced the *Jeannette* series and *La Serpentine* (Plates 116, 117). The five heads of the *Jeannette* series progress from a fairly faithful likeness of a girl's head to a much freer, broken style in which natural forms are expressively distorted. If *La Serpentine* does not reveal traditional ideas of classical beauty, it is nevertheless a rhythmic and forceful piece of sculpture, now recognized as one of Matisse's masterpieces.

117. *La Serpentine,* by Henri Matisse

Whereas Matisse's art has an intensely emotional effect on the spectator, that of Dufy is lighter in feeling and slighter in significance. In about 1918, after much experimentation, Dufy returned to a more delicate Fauve style and began to paint pictures with an elegant scurrying of line over bright-colored wash backgrounds. After World War II, he spent some time in the United States, a country that fascinated him. There he worked on paintings of crowds, skyscrapers, prairie sunsets, and Arizona rodeos. But for the greater part of his life, Dufy remained faithful to a few themes in his paintings. Devoted to music, he painted pictures in homage to Mozart and Bach (Plate 118) and delighted in painting orchestras, brass bands, and scenes at the opera (Plate 119). Other favorite subjects were the races and streets hung with bunting for celebrations. Dufy's work, if not so memorable as that of his more gifted and more serious contemporaries, always succeeds in captivating the spectator with its great charm.

André Derain's artistic career, like Dufy's, was launched as a Fauve. However, he was basically much more attracted to tradition than were most of his friends. He copied in the Louvre and never rejected the great painting of the past. The example of the past perhaps led Derain to be a more cautious painter than any other of the Fauves. His later pictures lack Fauve vitality, and he has none of the intellectual quality of Matisse. His are respectful paintings, and it was no doubt a respect for the ordered discipline of cubism that led him to be influenced by that movement; but he did not remain a cubist for long. The example of the early French and Italian "primitives" and the art of the fifteenth century came to dominate his imagination after about

118. *Homage to Bach,* by Raoul Dufy

119. *The Paris Opera House,* by Raoul Dufy

1920. Prior to that, the influence that classical painting had on his style can be seen in works such as *Two Sisters* (Plate 120). The pose of the two women is classical in attitude, but a new human sympathy is apparent in the treatment of these stark figures. It is to Derain's credit that, with so many different influences on his work, he managed to absorb them and yet keep a measure of his own individuality.

120. *Two Sisters,* by André Derain

IN THE YEARS before 1925 Picasso was applying the innovations of cubism and developing the style with ever-increasing strength. In 1917 he traveled to Rome, Naples, and Florence with the French "jack-of-all-arts" Jean Cocteau (1889–1963). This trip had two effects on Picasso. First, he became interested in *commedia dell'arte,* a traditional form of Italian theater in which the character Harlequin played a major role (Plate 121). Second, a deep appreciation for classical forms was revived in him. He began to paint many monumental female figures, either nude or in classical draperies. After the birth of his son in 1921, these impressive figures were often combined with others to portray the theme of motherhood.

Picasso next entered the phase of his career when he was associated in part with the surrealist movement. This movement, which we shall deal with presently, created a pictorial world of weird dreams and subconscious imagery. An example of this is Picasso's great *Figures on a Beach* (Plate 122). Although Picasso had entered the surrealist world of dreamlike relationships, his figures show certain cubist forms and colors, while the overall composition is classical in its grace.

The Muse (sometimes known as *Two Women;* Plate 123) is clearly a postcubist composition. In it, Picasso strives to reinterpret three-dimensionality; but its violent distortion is far more emotional, far less careful, than that of classical analytic cubism. The high point of this tendency is seen in *Guernica* (Plate 124), Picasso's passionate outcry against war. This greatest of all political paintings was produced during the

121. *Harlequin at the Looking Glass,* by Pablo Picasso

Spanish Civil War. Picasso was horrified at the ruthless attack by fascist bombers that completely destroyed the ancient Basque capital, Guernica. He found this action not only horribly inhuman but also profoundly contradictory to the whole of Spanish history and culture. Thus, it is the ancient animal symbols of Spain that spell out the terrible catastrophe, that raise the painting from protest against a single event to an artistic statement of timeless significance. The

122. *Figures on a Beach*, by Pablo Picasso

123. *The Muse*, by Pablo Picasso

gaping, disemboweled horse, the howling fleeing figures, the body of a dead soldier, and the anguished women become images of all human suffering.

Of social conscience, Picasso hotly declared in 1945:

> What do you think an artist is? An imbecile who has only his eyes if he's a painter, or ears if he's a musician, or a lyre at every level of his heart if he's a poet, or even if he's a boxer, just his muscles? On the contrary, he's at the same time a political being, constantly alive to heartrending, fiery or happy events, to which he responds in every way. How would it be possible to feel no interest in other people and by virtue of an ivory indifference to detach yourself from the life which they so copiously bring you? No, painting is not done to decorate apartments. It is an instrument of war for attack and defense against the enemy.[1]

This mood in Picasso's paintings continued throughout World War II. He was in Paris during the whole of the German occupation and refused to collaborate with the Vichy government or the Nazis in any way.

[1] In the light of Picasso's heroic statement, the works of two Mexican painters should be mentioned here—Diego Rivera (1886–1957) and David Alfaro Siqueiros (1898–   ). Mexico has long been known as a home of strong political passions. Rivera was able to combine politics and painting successfully in vast murals such as *The Mexican War of Independence* (Plate 125). Siqueiros, who led a students' strike at his art school at the age of fifteen, later joined the Mexican revolutionary army. He dedicated all his life to both painting and revolutionary politics, and for this he spent much time in prison. The furious character of his painting reflects the way he lived; certainly, *Echo of a Scream* (Plate 126) could not be more passionate in its message.

124. *Guernica* (detail), by Pablo Picasso

125. *The Mexican War of Independence*, by Diego Rivera

126. *Echo of a Scream*, by David Alfaro Siqueiros

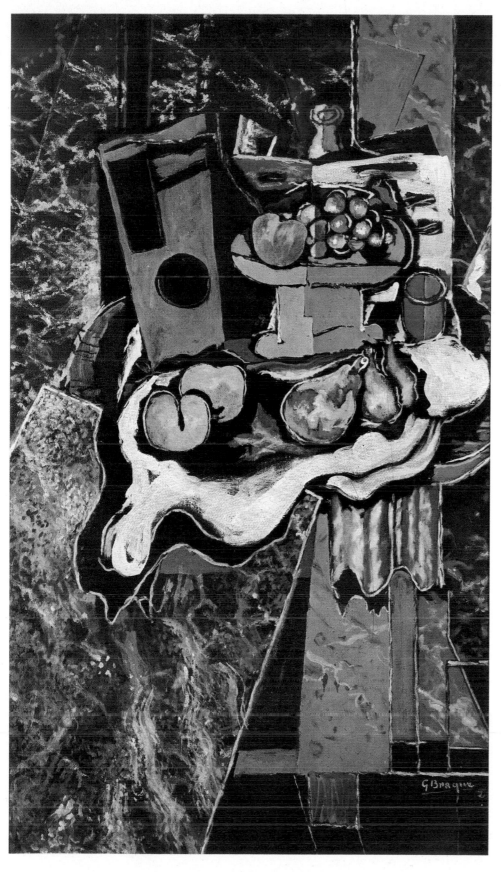

127. *Still Life on a Marble Table,* by Georges Braque

128. *Wheat Field*, by Georges Braque

129. *Soldiers Playing Cards*, by Fernand Léger

Before 1914, Picasso and Braque had lived and worked like Siamese twins but, as Picasso rather mysteriously said later, "When the mobilization started I sent Braque and Derain to the station. I have never seen them since." Thus an era ended. Braque was sent to the front, was wounded, and was commended for his bravery. He began painting again in 1917, but this time alone, for Picasso had moved far beyond him. Braque's cubism now became much freer and easier than before, particularly in his landscapes. His still lifes from this postwar period (Plate 127) are graceful in effect, with none of the hard, disciplined quality of the paintings of the classical analytic cubist period. Their color is more varied, and the drawing is more expressive. In his last years Braque developed still further. *Wheat Field* (Plate 128), a late work of 1952, shows an expres-

sive use of rich and heavy textures, with abstract tendencies very like post–World War II American painting.

Fernand Léger came in contact with cubism in 1910, the year that he met Picasso and Braque. He did not adopt their style, but borrowed from it. His simplifications have a special quality about them, a tooled metallic feeling; the different parts seem as if bolted together by an engineer (Plate 129). And indeed it was things like locomotive wheels, parts of complex machines, and bicycles that fascinated Léger. He had been drafted in 1914, and during the war he made many drawings of soldiers and weapons. These had a great effect on both his style and subject matter.

After 1921, human figures that did look as if made of iron began to play a larger role in his painting. These images, which

130. *Leisure: Homage to Louis David,* by Fernand Léger

never completely displaced machines in his work, are monumental and have an unnatural stability.

It was on his return to Paris from the United States after World War II that Léger completed the series *Leisure* (Plate 130). Popular pastimes had always attracted him as subject matter, and he did many paintings of cyclists (cycle racing then being the French national sport), as well as of soccer teams. Another similar, slightly later work is *The Great Parade* (Plate 131). In depicting such themes, as elsewhere, Léger participated in the life of his times and in modern discoveries with a kind of determined simplicity.

131. *The Great Parade*, by Fernand Léger

Chagall and Klee

EUROPEAN PAINTING, from the Renaissance through cubism, had been based on depiction of the visible world within the bounds of logic and normal perception. This long tradition meant absolutely nothing to Marc Chagall, and in his lopsided universe houses are built upside down, fish play the fiddle, and cows can fly.

Chagall was born in Vitebsk, a small Russian town in which half the population was Jewish. His childhood was filled with Jewish voices and Jewish faces, and in the tight community of small streets he could watch the dramas of the people around him. There were wedding processions, with musicians and dancing. There were market days when the Russian peasants would come in with their produce, bringing with them fields, skies, stars, and the warm vigor of people of the land. Chagall's family was poor. They ate herring, pickles, black bread and butter; and on the Sabbath his father, to young Marc's envy, would eat meat. Often there was only millet and barley meal to eat.

The feast days, with their colors and their banquets, deeply impressed Chagall, as did the candles for the dead climbing in a blaze toward the synagogue on the Day of Atonement. Most important of all to him was his family. It was large—aunts, uncles, and grandparents all being part of the family folklore that Chagall cherished in his imagination. On the throne of his family sat his energetic mother. His father was a quiet man whose smile, Chagall said, "whispered of the street where the dim passers-by roamed about, reflecting the moonlight."

There were others, such as Uncle Neuch, with whom Chagall used to ride and who played the violin like a gypsy (Plate 132). There was his grandfather, who spent half his life on top of the stove and who once was discovered sitting on the rooftop munching carrots. All these images were to provide Chagall with a lifetime's inspiration.

But in a Russian Jewish community it was impossible to become a painter; therefore Chagall, like Soutine, left for Paris. There he met the writer Max Jacob, Delaunay, Modigliani, and Apollinaire. The year in which Chagall arrived in Paris, 1910, was the same year in which Picasso completed his cubist masterpiece *Woman with a Mandolin*. The city's artistic life was then dominated by the experiments of the cubist painters. Chagall learned a firmer sense of form from these painters.

Chagall suffered greatly from homesickness in Paris. All the time he was there he continued to paint poetic, dreamlike memories of his native village. Of the paintings of this period, only *Paris through the Window* (Plate 133) takes the city as its subject and, moreover, betrays his uneasiness there. An atmosphere of muffled panic is felt. The double-faced man with the blue profile is masked, the sphynxlike cat registers alarm, and a train runs upside down. In the background are two small prone figures, seemingly knocked down or dead; above them, a parachutist descends perilously. Shafts of color, like searchlight beams, split the sky. The whole effect of this brightly hued picture is disturbing.

132. *The Green Violinist* (detail), by **Marc Chagall**

133. *Paris through the Window,* by Marc Chagall

Chagall left early in 1914 and went to Berlin for his first one-man exhibit. The outbreak of war sent him home to Vitebsk, where he married his adored Bella, the girl to whom he had been engaged before going to Paris. The birth of their daughter Ida in 1917 was the occasion for the brilliant and happy *Double Portrait with a Glass of Wine* (Plate 134). This is a superb picture of celebration, a picture with a laughing disregard for any established rules.

Suddenly, after the 1917 revolution, Chagall became a respected artistic figure in Russia. Offered a post as Minister of Arts, he preferred instead to return to Vitebsk in a lesser official capacity and founded a school of fine arts. Because he had no gift for administration or party politics, this episode ended in semicomic disaster—his pupils and professors finally rebelled and sent him packing to Moscow. There he was asked to do murals for the State Jewish Theater. These he executed in a revolutionary manner that gave free rein to his fantasy and imagination. With these works, he had arrived at his mature style.

Back in Paris in 1922, Chagall's color grew progressively richer. With increasing assurance, he started to play on the recurring themes that his intensely poetic imagination

134. *Double Portrait with a Glass of Wine,* by Marc Chagall

suggested to him. Acrobats, trapeze artists, and other circus performers became favorite subjects. There are also many paintings representing Bella and himself reclining or embracing amid enormous bouquets of flowers. *To My Wife* (Plate 135), a richly crowded composition, belongs to this series. Painted shortly after his wife died, it is both a tribute to her and a summary of his life's work.

Another painter remarkable for the charm and fantasy of his work was Paul Klee. He resembled Chagall in his mastery of an imaginative world which is childlike, rather than childish. While taking this seemingly unsophisticated approach to painting, Klee also was fully capable of dealing with adult emotions.

Klee took a long time to reach his mature style. He started in Munich and, under the influence of the decadent symbolism of Franz von Stuck (1863–1928), produced thin and wiry drawings reflecting turn-of-the-century German Jugendstil. From 1912, Klee was associated with the Blaue Reiter and became a close friend of its founders,

136. *The Red Balloon,* by Paul Klee

135. *To My Wife,* by Marc Chagall

Kandinsky and Marc. Through this association, he began to depend more on abstract form to express inner emotions. More important than his contact with the Blaue Reiter, perhaps, was his trip to Tunisia in 1914. He stayed only twelve days, but the rich visual experience of North Africa changed his attitudes radically. Previously he had concentrated on line and occasional watercolor washes. Now he was able to write in his diary, "Color and I are one: I am a painter."

Late in 1920 Klee was invited to teach at the Bauhaus in Weimar. This school of design had been founded the year before by the architect Walter Gropius. The Bauhaus curriculum wished to establish a closer relationship between architecture, the arts, and industrial design. In their own words, its members were attempting to "reestablish the harmony between the different artistic activities, between craftsmanship and artistry, and [to] bind them all together in a new conception of building." Klee taught there for ten years. With its reactionary official artistic policies, Nazi rule in Germany meant that the Bauhaus eventually had to close down (1933). Klee, who in 1931 had become a professor at the Düsseldorf Academy, was suspect for his modernism and was forced to return to his native Switzerland in 1933. He lived there until his death in 1940.

An early entry in Klee's diary gives a clue to the development of his career. In 1902 he wrote: "I want to be as though newborn, knowing nothing about Europe, nothing, knowing no pictures, entirely impulses, almost in an original state!" As an artist,

Klee was both very personal in his expression and socially oriented in aims. Very often his paintings are completely nonrepresentational or are composed of baffling forms whose meaning seems to escape us. An air of mystery is often strangely combined with his frankly childlike images (Plate 136). Furthermore, what may seem to be something breezily spontaneous in the finished work was actually calculated with extreme care by the artist.

137. *The Twittering Machine,* by Paul Klee

Klee described his drawing as "taking a line for a walk." Often his drawings are full of wit and humor. *The Twittering Machine* (Plate 137), for example, pokes fun at both mechanized society and the futurist movement. *Highways and Byways* (Plate 138), however, is an impression of an actual Egyptian landscape the artist visited on a trip in 1928–1929. Klee never failed to transform his gentle and almost faint outlines into forms that are highly meaningful.

138. *Highways and Byways,* by Paul Klee

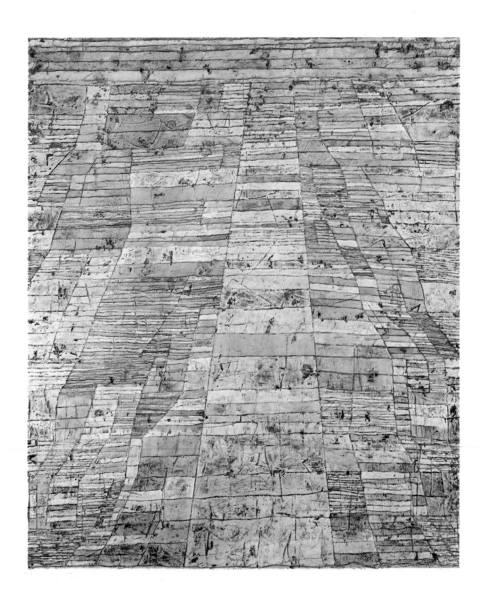

Morandi and Italian Metaphysical Painting

A FEELING for the mysterious significance of form is characteristic, in a different way, of the best paintings of the Italian painter Giorgio Morandi (1890–   ). This is particularly true of his haunting still lifes of bottles. His fellow-painter Giorgio de Chirico (1888–   ) wrote of Morandi, "He sees with the eyes of a man who believes; the inner framework of things that are dead for us, because motionless, appears to him under its most comforting aspect, under its eternal aspect." Morandi's more classic still lifes are almost always successful, particularly in his masterful handling of grainy textures (Plate 139). He has also painted a number of quiet and delicate landscapes (Plate 140); these and the still lifes have put him in the front rank of modern Italian painters. In some of his earlier works, there is evidence of the influence of the metaphysical painters (Plate 141).

Metaphysical painting was very largely an Italian development. (A formal definition of "metaphysics" is "the branch of philosophy which studies the ultimate nature of existence.") The driving force behind it was Giorgio de Chirico. The painting of this school is at its best when closest to the blank, airless, somehow menacing atmosphere of *Nostalgia of the Poet* and *Enigma of the Hour* (Plates 142, 143). The emphasis in metaphysical painting on empty streets, abandoned railway stations, and a general feeling of being lost or out of place can be traced back to De Chirico and the circumstances of his youth.

Giorgio de Chirico spent the first years of his life in Greece, where his father was supervising the construction of a railroad line. There he received some elementary lessons in art, but he produced little to suggest that he was exceptionally talented. Returning to Italy after his father's death, he moved from city to city. He was always in his mother's company and never stayed in any one place for long.

It was in Paris that he began to make out what he described as "the first ghosts of a more complete, more profound and more complicated art, an art which was—in one word—more *metaphysical*." His paintings were now concerned with empty streets,

139. *Still Life,* by Giorgio Morandi

140. *Landscape,* by Giorgio Morandi

141. *Still Life with Manikin,* by Giorgio Morandi

144. *Hector and Andromache,* by Giorgio de Chirico

143. *Enigma of the Hour,* by Giorgio de Chirico

142. *Nostalgia of the Poet,*
by Giorgio de Chirico

145. *The Hermaphrodite Idol,* by Carlo Carrà

this time, also, that manikins first appeared in his work. These manikins bear a strong resemblance to the jointed ones used by artists for sketching proportions or physical movement. In the paintings they become creatures with no human concerns, yet are an eerie kind of second-hand approximation of human forms (Plate 144).

The war again forced the De Chirico family to return to Italy, and Giorgio was drafted into the Italian army. Confined to a military hospital, he met Carlo Carrà (already discussed in connection with the futurist movement). Carrà's enthusiasm for that determinedly dynamic style had died down, and he was ready for a change. Painting side by side with De Chirico in the hospital, he adopted the metaphysical style (Plate 145). An entertaining note is that the staff doctors thought they might be off their heads.

Carrà took over many motifs (specific themes or subjects) from De Chirico, as did Morandi, briefly the third member of their group. But neither of them was able to develop the metaphysical style any further. Nor, it would seem, could De Chirico himself; his later work grew flabby and lacked the power of his earlier fantasies. When he started to reinterpret the masters of the Renaissance, his once devoted followers the surrealists (champions of fantastic art) turned on him. In their 1928 exhibition, having called him a coward, a cheat, and a viper, the younger painters assembled a model entitled *Here Lies Giorgio de Chirico.* This was a cheap plaster reproduction of the leaning tower of Pisa surrounded by little rubber horses and doll furniture. These spiteful references to certain themes in De Chirico's work show the mixture of malice and childishness typical of many of the quarrels within surrealist groups.

gloomy statuary, puzzling figures and situations. The emphasis was always on desertion. Human beings scarcely exist in De Chirico's art. He shows us only the shell of life—man-made objects and inanimate beings from whom human feeling has been mystifyingly stripped away.

These unusual landscapes were followed, about the time of the outbreak of World War I, by a concentration on a hodgepodge of objects such as gloves, cigar boxes, and hands from anatomical models. It was at

Dada

WHAT THE word *Dada* means, or who made it up, remains obscure to this day. This would have appealed to the originators of the movement, who, in 1916, gathered together in Zurich at the Café Voltaire. Like surrealism, the movement was as much concerned with literature as with painting. Its originators, exiles and refugees, were equally rootless.

The Café Voltaire group was founded by Hugo Ball (1886–1927), a German writer who later became a religious recluse. He was joined by the jovial Romanian poet Tristan Tzara (1896–1968) and the painters Jean Arp (1887–1966) and Marcel Janco (1895–   ). Their method was to shock, and their aim was to lead an artistic revolt that would question the basis and deny the very existence of art.

Meetings at the Café Voltaire featured music and songs, and also such novelties as poems composed only of vowels. Absurd and only partly planned performances—the ancestors of today's "happenings"—broke out regularly. From this volatile background came the magazine *Dada*, which was almost entirely the creation of Tzara. The typography was scattered haphazardly across the page, and while the magazine had a certain flair, its editorial policy was to be against everything, no matter what. Thus the Dada manifesto tiresomely proclaimed: "Dada means nothing!" Other irksome discoveries included such axioms as "Thought is produced in the mouth." Typical Dada poems, shrieked or bellowed at the top of the lungs to startled audiences, had such memorable lines as "gadji beri bimba glandridi lanla louni caltori."

This forthright rejection of all the accepted standards of the European cultural tradition spread from Zurich to Berlin, Cologne, and Paris, and finally to New York. Dada had a surprisingly profound effect on the painting—or rather, "anti-painting—of the time.

In Cologne, Kurt Schwitters (1887–1948) founded his own branch of Dada, which he called "Merz" ("rubbish"). He constructed his art from bits and pieces found in the streets. Streetcar tickets, broken shoelaces, dirty feathers, wrapping paper—anything that had been thrown away as useless he collected avidly and transformed into collages (Plate 146). Their creation was his most important artistic activity, but he also wrote poetry and plays and tirelessly publicized Dada.

As a thoroughgoing rejecter of the world's standards, Francis Picabia (1879–1953) should have received some kind of special award. He was rich, rootless, eccentric, and quite frankly unable to see any meaning in the world or in art. Art, he said, must be "useless and impossible."

Picabia had nothing but sneering contempt for painting and for those who respected it. A talented painter as a child, he replaced his grandfather's old masters with his own copies; he then sold the originals to raise funds to enlarge his stamp collection. Later, he began attaching meaningless titles such as *Edtaonise* to his paintings and proclaimed that the title had more value than the picture. This was not the case, however, with *L'Enfant Carburateur* ("The Baby Carburetor"; Plate 147). Here the carefully balanced abstract structure and the precision of the diagram disguise just one slight flaw: namely, that this machine has no meaning or no practical function whatsoever.

146. *Composition,* by Kurt Schwitters

147. *L'Enfant Carburateur,* by Francis Picabia

In Barcelona, he produced his own Dada periodical called *391* (once again, named for no particular reason). It contained not only his own restless semimechanical drawings but also poems by Apollinaire and Max Jacob and cubist drawings by Picasso and Braque. The police ran Picabia out of Spain. Without a backward glance he departed for America, where he was met by his old friend Marcel Duchamp, the greatest of all Dada artists.

Duchamp's association with Dada became suddenly apparent when he rejected his Section d'Or tradition by mounting a bicycle wheel on a wooden chair. This flash of inspiration was followed by his painting a moustache and an obscene pun on a reproduction of the *Mona Lisa.* Next, he exhibited such objects as a bottle rack, a hat stand, and a shovel. These last were all ordinary manufactured items, generally bought on sale, which Duchamp merely signed. Needless to say, their exhibition brought into question exactly what could be considered art. Duchamp simply called them his "ready-mades."

At the same time that he was collecting these articles and transforming them, merely by choosing them, into "ready-mades," Duchamp was embarking on his major work. This was the famous *Bride Stripped Bare by her Bachelors, Even* (Plate 148), an extremely complicated work that took twelve years to bring to what Duchamp called "a state of final incompletion." It consisted of two large sheets of glass, to which were added oil paint, lead wire, foil, dust, and varnish. Typically, he announced that the painting was "finished" only when it was accidentally cracked in 1926.

After this "anti-triumph" of anti-art, Duchamp gave up his artistic activities in favor of chess and very rarely produced new works. These later works also show him to be one of the most prophetic artists of this century, for in his whirling *Rotoreliefs* (1935) and *Fluttering Hearts* (1936) he anticipated both kinetic art and "pop" art by several decades.

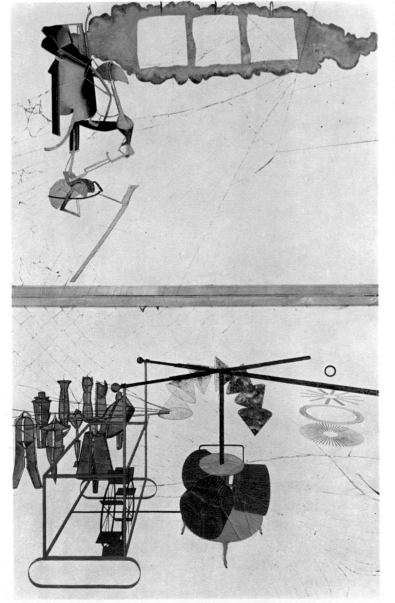

Surrealism

ANDRÉ BRETON (1896–1966), Louis Aragon (1897–   ), and Philippe Soupault (1897–   )—none of them more than twenty-five years old at the time—were responsible for the first outbreak of surrealism in Paris. Together these three young poets ran the magazine *Littérature*, which was itself a fairly traditional journal. Dada had made an impact on their imaginations and led them to start their own rebellion. They broke with the Dadaists because they could not accept Dada's waywardness and anarchy.

The new group subscribed wholeheartedly to the values of dream worlds, folly, and madness. They were convinced that deliberate rejection of logical processes of thought and artistic creation would lead to a new kind of art. "We are still living under the reign of logic," complained Breton in the first surrealist manifesto in 1924. It was a reign that he felt to be tyrannical. "I believe," he continued, "in the future transmutation [i.e., synthesis] of those two seemingly contradictory states, dream and reality, into a sort of absolute reality of *surreality,* so to speak." The word "surrealism" had been coined previously by Apollinaire.

True freedom of the imagination was to be found both in the intense, feverish visions of such surrealist heroes as the poets Arthur Rimbaud and Gérard de Nerval, or in the world of dreams. Poetry and painting alike should be irrational and should shock or

148. *The Bride Stripped Bare by Her Bachelors, Even,* by Marcel Duchamp

149. *The Eye of Silence,* by Max Ernst

startle the senses. "Beauty," said Breton, "will be convulsive or it will not be."

Breton had studied medicine and worked with mentally disturbed soldiers during World War I. Freud's psychological theories and discoveries he knew well. Sometimes during analysis, the military patients had been encouraged to daydream and play free-association word games; and Breton thought these methods could be used in artistic creation. He described how he came to make his first experiments in this direction. As he was dropping off to sleep one night, he heard a curious phrase, "as if it had knocked on the window-pane." Something said to him distinctly, "There's a man cut in two by the window." This was followed up by a clear visual impression of the unfortunate incident. Soon after, Breton began writing whatever came into his head—on good days, fifty pages at a time.

Sharing Breton's unusual opinions was Max Ernst (1891–   ), a painter who, as he obscurely phrased it, tried to express in his work "the irritation of my visionary faculties." Ernst was the first true surrealist artist.

In 1922, using what amounted to a Dada technique, Ernst began creating collages with scraps of illustrations from old books. He believed these chance combinations could give a poetic reinterpretation of the real world. He welcomed hallucinations. In 1925, as he was staring at the wood-grain swirls of a hotel floor, strange images appeared to him. He placed sheets of paper on the floor and rubbed over them with graphite. (Rubbings like these are called "frottages"; by putting a piece of paper on a penny and rubbing over it with a pencil, anybody can make one.) Looking at these, Ernst said, "I was surprised by the sudden strengthening of my visionary faculties and by hallucinatory sequence of images." This deliberate release from the real world led to the terrifying landscapes of his most typical work. *The Eye of Silence* (Plate 149) shows an unearthly region that seems to be covered with a veil of fungus or evil moss. *The Anti-Pope* (Plate 150) combines the fine, gritty precision of coral formations with a menacing decay.

Joan Miró (1893–) is a lighter and happier painter in a more or less surrealist vein. Commuting between his native Barcelona and Paris in the years before 1925, he absorbed the examples of cubism, Kandinsky's abstractions, and Klee's highly personal childlike forms. These influences helped to form Miró's distinctive style—a style of great freedom and poetic, playful associations (Plates 151, 152). But it was his contacts with the surrealists that had a decisive influence on his art. Miró never numbered actively among the surrealists, although he was often associated with their movement. From them Miró learned the value of the subconscious, and in his works he often achieves what Breton had called the basic aim of surrealism: uniting the

"surreal" (a combination of supernatural and subconscious imagery) with the real. Even Miró's most outlandish figures give the impression of inhabiting the real world. This was true also of his fellow-Spaniard Picasso during the brief phase when his work was influenced by the surrealists, as may be seen in his *Figures on a Beach* (Plate 122).

The best-known of the surrealists is yet another Spaniard, Salvador Dali (1904–), an extroverted and self-publicizing artist. As a child he had been wild, talented, and impossibly spoiled. Indulged by his parents, he was permitted to do whatever he liked, whenever he liked. The young Dali was expelled as a show-off from every art school he attended; somehow, this did not disturb the course of his artistic development. At the San Fernando Institute in Madrid, he met the great Spanish poet Federico García Lorca and the film director Luis Buñuel, with whom Dali was later to create an artistic uproar. In 1923 he was thrown out of the institute for inciting a rebellion. In the same year he came across some reproductions of the works of De Chirico and Carrà in the Italian magazine *Valori Plastici*. The mysteriousness of their metaphysical painting gave him a new artistic impulse.

As decisive as this discovery were his trips to Paris in 1927 and 1928. Visited by Paul Eluard and his wife Gala at his home in Cadaqués, Spain, Dali fell in love with Gala and eventually married her. Back in Paris, in 1928–1930, Dali collaborated with his friend Buñuel in making some of the first surrealist films, *Un Chien andalou* and *L'Age d'or* ("An Andalusian Dog" and "The Golden Age"). Both were brought out with as much surrealist fanfare as possible, and the scandalous nature of the films increased the public furor. *L'Age d'or*, the

150. *The Anti-Pope,* by Max Ernst

151. *Large Composition,* by Joan Miró

152. *Man and Dog in Front of the Sun,* by Joan Miró

first feature-length surrealist film (in which Max Ernst starred as the leader of a band of outlaws), was sabotaged at its première by a right-wing political group. At a given signal, ink bottles were thrown at the screen, the audience was assaulted, and paintings by Dali, Miró, Ernst, and Yves Tanguy were trampled underfoot.

Surrealism thrived on such events. Its public image needed continual feeding by such personalities as Dali, who wore extraordinary clothes and a waxed moustache like a pitchfork and gave lectures at the university with one foot soaking in a bowl of ass's milk. He could always be relied on not to behave conventionally.

Dali's best and most characteristic surrealist period came when he returned to Spain with Gala. There they settled at Port Lligat, a tiny, poverty-stricken fishing village. Dali rented a shack from a crazed old fisherwoman named Lydia, who appears in many of his paintings of the time. In these paintings he set about transforming and intensifying the poverty, madness, and violence of the village. He turned the steep rocks and harsh sunsets into deeply receding landscapes of a black-magic world. In this frightening surrealist world, giraffes burn, half-eaten telephones lie on the beach, and pocket watches melt in the unnatural heat. Looming above, disturbing shapes disfigure the calm of the sky (Plate 153). All these strange elements were painted in a minutely realistic way.

Following sharp disagreements with Breton, Dali divorced himself from the surrealist movement. He continued to paint in much the same general manner, but with increasingly weaker effect. His landscape backgrounds, empty and haunted, were derived from the paintings of Yves Tanguy (1900–1955), who was an early member of the surrealist group. Entirely self-taught, Tanguy began painting in 1924 when he saw one of De Chirico's works. His great theme was the infinity of space. In *Fear* (Plate 154) one cannot even guess at distance from or over the horizon, for the horizon itself does not exist. This is an authentic pictorial representation of a mystery. Tanguy found that he could only people his strange landscapes with inhuman forms. Sometimes these have an uncanny resemblance to Jean Arp's shapes. Compare, for instance, Tanguy's *Palace on a Promontory* with Arp's *Configuration* (Plates 155, 156).

If Tanguy seems to have constructed a totally different universe, the Belgian René Magritte (1898–1967), instead, subtly introduces peculiar elements into the affairs of everyday life. He is more concerned with showing how near the surreal is to ordinary life than with Breton's attitude of meshing the real and the surreal. His quietly menacing pictures seem full of warnings or premonitions. The *Voice of the Winds* (Plate 157) is so calm and assured in its somewhat "science fiction" matter-of-factness that we are forced to believe in what we see. He also indulged in surrealistic parody on occasion, with witty references to earlier paintings, sometimes spoofing them (Plate 158).

Magritte had a family history of suicides and nervous depressions. He studied at the Brussels Academy of Fine Arts and later took a job designing hideous wallpapers for Belgian living rooms. His free time he spent painting in his own way. After seeing the work of the Parisian surrealists, he moved to Paris and worked there from 1927 until 1930. Had his output during those years been greater, it is likely that he would have become the most distinguished of the surrealist painters.

153. *Premonition of Civil War,*
by Salvador Dali

154. *Fear,* by Yves Tanguy

155. *Palace on a Promontory,* by Yves Tanguy

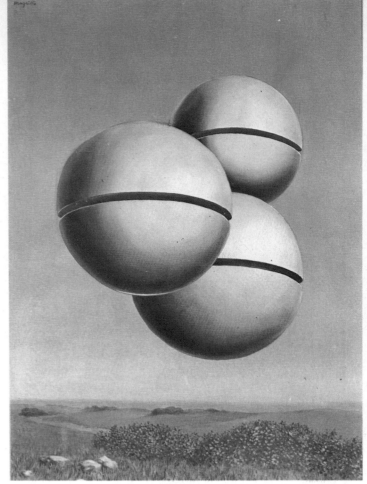

157. *Voice of the Winds,* by René Magritte

158. *Perspective: Madame Récamier of Gérard,* by René Magritte

156. *Configuration,* by Jean Arp

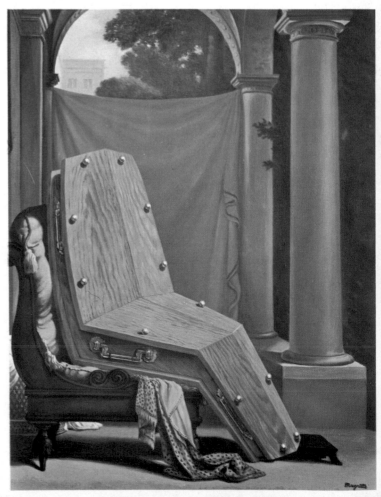

Sculpture

TWO SCULPTORS made significant contributions to the surrealist movement. Having first studied in Strasbourg, Jean (Hans) Arp came into contact with Parisian art in 1904. His style was formed, however, by association with the Blaue Reiter group in Munich. He knew Apollinaire and his circle, and in 1916 Arp helped found the Dada movement in Zurich. He then worked with Max Ernst in Cologne. Arp did not concentrate his attention on sculpture until 1930. Even when he comes closest to representing the human figure, there is often a suggestion of organic vegetable form in his work (Plates 159, 160). Arp's sculptures resemble one another in the subtle flow of one curved plane into another. His paintings are more surrealist in their suggestive forms than is his austere sculpture.

Alberto Giacometti (1901–1966), the son of a Swiss postimpressionist painter, came to artistic maturity in neither Dada nor surrealist circles. He had studied with the restrained and classical French sculptor Aristide Maillol (1861–1944). He did not first meet the surrealists until 1930. Although his association with them was brief, it did produce such authentically surrealist works as the *Table* (Plate 161). This extraordinary article, neither sculpture nor furniture, is reminiscent of Dali's fondness for designing chairs that were impossible to sit on.

In later years, Giacometti became increasingly preoccupied with themes of loneliness and isolation. *The Piazza* (Plate 162) is composed of five freestanding figures with no apparent interplay as individuals. Their elongated skeletal proportions are a Giacometti trademark. In *The Forest* (Plate 163)

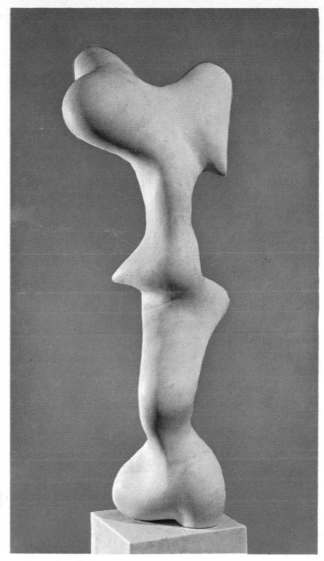

159. *Growth,* by Jean Arp

160. *Human Concretion,* by Jean Arp

161. *Table,* by Alberto Giacometti

163. *The Forest,* by Alberto Giacometti

162. *The Piazza,* by Alberto Giacometti

loneliness is grimly expressed by an isolated detailed face set in a forest of coldly silent semihuman figures.

Emile Antoine Bourdelle (1869–1929), like many sculptors, entered on his artistic career as a result of working in another craft during his youth. His father was a carpenter and cabinetmaker, and the young boy began by helping to carve the ornamental parts on sideboards made by his father. Bourdelle attended the Toulouse École des Beaux-Arts and subsequently went on to the École des Beaux-Arts in Paris. Finding the academic disciplines there too strict, however, he left after only a few months. In 1893 Bourdelle became an assistant to Rodin and remained with him for some fifteen years. Undoubtedly, to have been in continuous contact with the greatest sculptor of the age was very inspiring; yet it is possible that it also prevented Bourdelle from fully developing as a sculptor in his own right. His own personality might easily have become subdued by that of the greater man.

In his first period Bourdelle's work is very similar to that of Rodin. The series of portraits of Beethoven (Plate 164), however, have enough force and decision to be considered as independent creations. Bourdelle's monumental style was remarkable in its ability to treat great themes with power and control, even when he worked on a comparatively small scale. This power can be seen in his well-known *Hercules Aiming at the Stymphalian Birds* (Plate 165).

By contrast, Aristide Maillol appears to have been interested in poise rather than in movement. His style varied little throughout his career, perhaps because he was already thirty-five when he became a sculptor. Earlier, he had pursued a career as a painter (he had been in contact with Gauguin and the Nabis in 1893), and then as a weaver

164. *Beethoven on the Rocks,*
by Emile Antoine Bourdelle

165. *Hercules Aiming at the Stymphalian Birds,*
by Emile Antoine Bourdelle

of tapestries. Although he did a fine bust of Renoir (Plate 166), Maillot's talents as a sculptor did not lie in the field of portraiture. All his work seems to be an attempt to avoid striking personality in an effort to be stately and monumental. His classical-looking nudes, which make up the greater part of his output, are somewhat static and generally over-life-size figures. Their ample bodies often have a certain thickness about them, like that of the *Venus with a Necklace* (Plate 167), and their placid faces are bare of human emotion.

There are similar objections to the sculpture of Charles Despiau (1874–1946). His masterpiece, the delicate *Paulette* (Plate 168), is not at all representative of his prevailing style. This work brought him to Rodin's attention, and Despiau became an assistant to the older sculptor for some time. In the end, however, Despiau seemed incapable of taking anything from his master, and he remained more or less academic and workmanlike in his own art.

Active also as a graphic artist and playwright, the German expressionist Ernst Barlach (1870–1938) is most noted for his compassionate sculpture. From his decora-

166. *Renoir,* by Aristide Maillol

167. *Venus with a Necklace,* by Aristide Maillol

tive Jugendstil (Art Nouveau) early style he went on, after contact with early Van Gogh and Millet paintings and with Russian folk religion, to develop an earthy yet monumental style that owed much to medieval metalcraft and woodcarving. He revived this latter, little-used technique, and its qualities influenced him even when he worked in stone. Through all his subjects, mostly beggars or other suffering figures, there runs a current of emotional mysticism that is in strange contrast to their robust proportions (Plate 169).

Another individual and gifted German sculptor of this era was Wilhelm Lehmbruck (1881–1919), whose academic beginnings and interest in Rodin's and Maillol's figure studies are evident in his later, more personal work. His career was ended prematurely when, at the age of thirty-eight and in ill health, he committed suicide. He was chiefly concerned with the nude figure, and in his best-known works—such as his meditative *Kneeling Woman* of 1911 (Plate 170) —he exhibits a graceful style recalling qualities of both Art Nouveau and late Gothic sculpture.

The sculptor Constantin Brancusi (1876–1957) was by nature a man continually searching for the new. He left home at the age of eleven to explore the world, abandoning his father's Romanian farm for years of vagabondage, during which he wandered all over Eastern Europe. By 1898 he was back in Romania, at the Bucharest Art Academy, where he received several years of formal training in drawing and sculpture before arriving in Paris sometime after 1900. In that year the great dominating star of the world of sculpture was, of course, Rodin. No young sculptor could fail to be influenced by him, and the heads that Brancusi produced in his first years in Paris were very

168. *Paulette,* by Charles Despiau

170. *Kneeling Woman,* by Wilhelm Lehmbruck

169. *Man Singing,* by Ernst Barlach

like those of Rodin. But not only did the great sculptor influence the young—he had a tendency to swallow them whole. Sculptors such as Despiau who went to work for him as assistants never again produced any work with strong individual value and significance.

This was a fate that Brancusi avoided. An invitation to join Rodin at Meudon was refused. Brancusi quickly turned down the offer, an arrangement that would have made him financially comfortable. This he did not only through pride in his own independence, but through a deep realization that the whole method and the whole effect of Rodin's sculpture had to be abandoned. Brancusi disliked Rodin's smudged impressionistic modeling, his romanticism, and his frequent sentimental theatricality. This style had to be replaced by sculpture of clean outlines, in which there was nothing superfluous. The new sculpture must seem pared down rather than built up; it must be classical in its purity and restraint even if it was not classical in its forms.

Thus Brancusi took to producing such works as the *Maiastra* and *Sleeping Muse* (Plates 171, 172). The maiastra is a bird in a Romanian folktale which guides a lover through the forest to his imprisoned princess, thereby ensuring her release and their future happiness. The *Sleeping Muse* shares with several other of Brancusi's sculptures a tendency toward the elemental shape of the egg, revealing again his persistent concern with completely basic outlines.

Brancusi's early years in Paris were a time of stimulating contact with other artists. Modigliani especially was a close friend, and it was Brancusi who first encouraged him to try sculpture. Another friend was Henri Rousseau, for whose tomb Brancusi later carved a monumental pillar. He exhibited fairly frequently at the Salon d'Automne,

171. *The Maiastra*, by Constantin Brancusi

172. *Sleeping Muse,* by Constantin Brancusi

173. *The Rooster,*
by Constantin Brancusi

sometimes with a startling effect on the public. Like so many other artists of his time, Brancusi was continually troubled by the public's failure to understand his work. He was involved for years in a lawsuit with the United States Customs Service, which refused to admit one of his works into America duty-free, as a work of art. They insisted that it was not a work of art, but merely a piece of polished metal and therefore taxable. It may have been incidents such as these which drove Brancusi into increasing isolation.

During World War I, Brancusi developed an interest in creating rough-hewn wood images like totem poles (Plate 173). One such piece is *The Rooster*. Despite Brancusi's denials, these sculptures seem to have been inspired by primitive and exotic art. The wood carvings he created after the war, for example, *Adam and Eve* (Plate 174), became increasingly abstract. The totem-pole element in his work was developed to a surprising degree in his imposing *Endless Column*, which rises to a height of 98 feet. This daring and lovely sculpture, cast in gilded steel, was erected near his birthplace, at Târgu-Jiu, where it lends a disconcerting science-fiction touch to the wooded Carpathian landscape.

Antoine Pevsner (1886–1962) was born into a family of refinery engineers in Russia. This family background seems to have influenced strongly his direction as an artist. While his brother went to work in a copper refinery, Antoine attended the Kiev Academy of Fine Arts for several years. After arriving in Paris in 1913, he became friendly with Modigliani and Archipenko and soon produced his first abstract painting.

From Paris, Pevsner went to Oslo, where he stayed from 1915 to 1917. This was to prove a most important period for him. In Oslo he was joined by his brother, Naum Gabo (1890–   ). While continuing to paint, Pevsner became more and more interested in his brother's sculpture and, finally, started to sculpt himself. The two brothers began to evolve a totally new kind of sculpture—new in that it began to use space itself as an integral part of the work of art (Plate 175), gradually leading to the abandonment of traditional principles of building sculpture out of compact masses. These revolutionary ideas were further developed during Pevsner's period as a teacher at the Moscow Higher Art and Technical School, where he was in continual contact with such artists as Kandinsky and Malevich.

In the wake of the Russian Revolution, both brothers signed the *Realist Manifesto*, which was printed by the revolutionary government in August, 1920, and posted all over Moscow. This document, which was of the greatest importance to modern sculpture, admirably summed up the guiding principles behind its development. The opening statement read, "If art is to be a reflection of real life, it should be based on two fundamental factors: space and time." Next, "Volume is not the only means of expressing space." The manifesto ended by declaring that "Art must cease to be imitative and must invent new forms."

About this time, the word "constructivist" was first used with reference to the brothers' work. Under the constructivist banner, Pevsner went to Berlin in 1922 with a government-sponsored exhibition of modern Russian art. He stayed in Germany for some months and then went on to Paris, where he finally made the decision to give up painting and devote himself to sculpture.

In 1924 the two brothers held a joint exhibition at the Galerie Percier in Paris, an exhibition that helped to make the direction their art was taking more definite and precise.

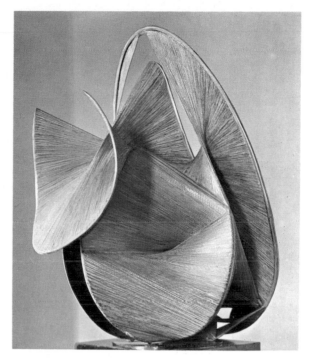

175. *Construction in an Egg,* by Antoine Pevsner

174. *Adam and Eve,* by Constantin Brancusi

Pevsner's experiments with space and perspective led him to the use of transparent materials and to great freedom in combining open planes. Often his materials were varied: his *Portrait of Marcel Duchamp* (New Haven, Conn., Yale University Art Gallery), made of plates of zinc, copper, and celluloid, shows a clever use of contrast. In his later years, his work shows both clarity and purpose—a purposefulness and application that are also to be seen in the hard, craggy sculpture of the Spaniard Julio González (1876–1942).

González came from Barcelona; his father, a coppersmith, taught him to work in metal while he was studying at art school. But at this time of his life and in the years after 1900, when the whole family moved to Paris, González' main interest lay in painting. He produced heavy, somber canvases that were of little merit. When he finally took to sculpture, he worked, significantly, in iron. His metal sculpture is clearly the sculpture of a blacksmith.

Having learned acetylene welding at the Renault automobile factory, González went on to larger and more ambitious works. The iron was riveted and forged with a power that seems to surge through his compositions. In works such as the *Woman Combing Her Hair* (Plate 176) he was, like Pevsner, concerned with a new type of sculptural composition. As he himself said, the aim was "to project space and draw in it, with the help of new mediums: to use this space and build with it, as if it were a newly discovered medium—that is my whole endeavor." In this, González achieved a great deal of success. Despite a life of poverty and unhappiness, which was largely spent in solitude, his output shows how right such

176. *Woman Combing Her Hair,* by Julio González

other sculptors as Brancusi and Gargallo were to encourage and support him (Plate 177).

Pablo Gargallo (1881–1934) was another Spaniard, and one who also began at the art academy in Barcelona. In 1901 he shared a studio there with Picasso, and worked with him again when he went to Paris in 1906. The achievements of cubism in painting made Gargallo realize that sculpture lagged far behind. Although his style was basically traditional, Gargallo made certain advances in the art. Like González, he used iron. Although he was no true constructor of space, he did develop a technique, seen here in *Maternity* (Plate 178), which was new and which has since been influential in the work of other artists. The basic trick of this technique was to translate convex planes into concave, and vice versa.

Gargallo helped his old friend Picasso when, in 1931, he decided to sculpt in metal. Gargallo was invited to Picasso's château at Boisgeloup to teach him the necessary techniques, and in the next year Picasso produced a large number of metal sculptures.

Two Eastern Europeans made individual contributions to the sculpture of the modern period. Ossip Zadkine (1890–1967) was sent from Russia, at the age of sixteen, to finish his education in, of all places, Sunderland, England. There he began to draw and sculpt at evening classes and then went to London, where he moved in literary and artistic circles. Far more decisive to his art was his move to Paris in 1909, where he immediately took to cubism. At this stage his work was more obviously cubist than that of any other sculptor; but these early works do not compare in quality with those

177. *Monserrat,* by Julio González

of his maturity, such as the great Rotterdam monument (Plate 179), which commemorates with great force the destruction of Rotterdam by the Nazis.

Jacques Lipchitz arrived in Paris from his native Lithuania in the same year as Zadkine, and was similarly impressed with cubism. But his reaction to it was more timid, and his early attempts to translate the new language of painting into stone lacked power.

It took him some time to find a personal style. He eventually achieved this by reducing his figures to their essential elements, producing at first a rather awkward effect. A later style, to which *Sacrifice II* and *Return of the Son* (Plates 180, 181) belong, has an assured sense of movement and an effective ability to construct in contours.

Still another significant sculptor who began his long career in this same period

178. *Maternity,* by Pablo Gargallo

179. *Monument Commemorating the Destruction of Rotterdam,* by Ossip Zadkine

140

was Jacob Epstein (1880–1959). Born in New York of Polish Jewish parents, he worked first in a foundry; then, having emigrated, in 1902 he went to the École Nationale des Beaux-Arts and the Académie Julian in Paris. After this rather brief stay in Paris, he settled permanently in London, where his distinctive style shocked and at times enraged the British public from that time on. Eighteen statues commissioned by the British Medical Association first put him outside the pale of ordinary middle-class opinion. This was the beginning of an alienation that troubled him all his life, although he never lacked commissions for his sculptures. Early in his career, probably in 1911, he was commissioned to do a statue for the tomb of Oscar Wilde, the famous English playwright and poet, in the Père La Chaise cemetery in Paris. This work

180. *Sacrifice II,* by Jacques Lipchitz

181. *Return of the Son,* by Jacques Lipchitz

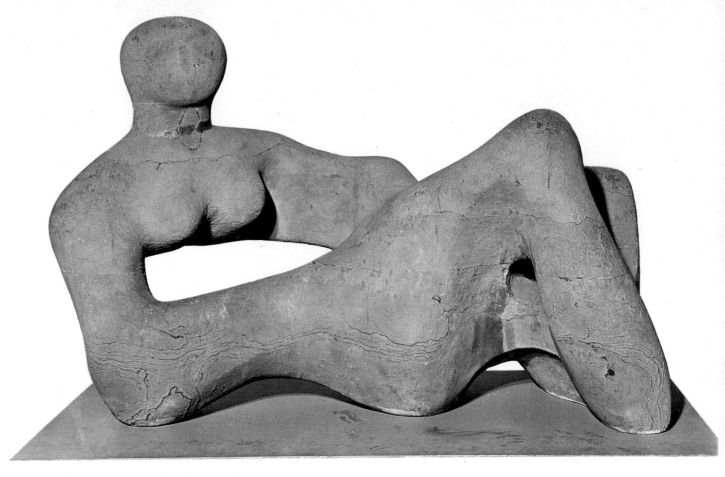

184. *Reclining Figure,* by Henry Moore

182. *The Visitation,* by Sir Jacob Epstein   183. *Selina,* by Sir Jacob Epstein

already reveals the firm individuality of his sculptural imagination. Over the tomb he constructed a huge, heavy, sphinx-like figure of an angel. A very unusual angel it was, indeed, with an expression of puffy dissipation and heavy bags under its eyes. When the statue was set in position, the public and authorities howled in outrage. It was during the commotion of this period that Epstein first came into contact with Picasso, Modigliani, and Brancusi.

Later, Epstein modeled his famous *Visitation* (Plate 182). The extent to which public disapproval had worried Epstein can be gathered from his comment at the time: "This figure stands with folded hands, and expresses a humility so profound as to shame the beholder who comes to my sculpture expecting rhetoric or splendor of gesture. This work alone refutes all the charges of

185. *Warrior,* by Henry Moore

blatancy and self-advertisement leveled at me."

Epstein perhaps excelled as a religious sculptor. In this field he could effectively combine his intensely expressionistic style and his feeling for symbolic figures in a more traditional style. But his standard of portraiture was also very high, as seen in the bust *Selina* (Plate 183), which portrays his cleaning woman. Epstein's large-scale works are extremely stirring. These include his *War Memorial,* a powerful statement against war, and *St. Michael and the Devil,* a dramatic sculpture for Coventry Cathedral.

The British sculptor Henry Moore (1898–) is one of the major artists of our time, a superb craftsman and also a man of profound and complex vision. Born in Yorkshire, he first studied teaching and became an artist only after World War I. He had received some measure of recognition in England by 1928, when he was commissioned to make a relief for the St. James's underground (subway) station. At that time he usually worked by direct carving of stone or wood; as Michelangelo had felt before him, Moore believed that form lay concealed in the material, awaiting only the sculptor's revealing labor. Moore's respect and love for carving has provided the basis of his style. He is always aware of the solidity and heaviness of stone and of the grain and structure of wood, in working with those materials. After 1945, he began to work more in bronze. But the language of forms he had evolved over the years of carving by hand remained remarkably unchanged; only the surface texture was now different.

Throughout his life Moore has concentrated on a few themes, themes of extreme simplicity. These are mostly concerned with the human body—standing, sitting, or, more

186. *The Rocking Chair,*
by Henry Moore

187. *Two Figures (Menhir),* by Barbara Hepworth

188. *Two Standing Figures,* (1950) by Kenneth Armitage

144

often, reclining (Plate 184). The single human figure has been a frequent subject in modern sculpture, often meant to express a feeling of tragic isolation. In Moore's work the single figure is quite different; it is vital, even in repose, with every contour emphasizing the life force (Plate 185). When Moore groups figures, they create an organic relationship.

After the reclining woman, the theme to which he most often returned was that of the mother and child. During World War II he did many drawings in the London bomb shelters. These drawings often featured shrouded women with children (Plate 186). When commissioned to make a Madonna and Child group after the war, he made a long series of preliminary studies for it. In these he incorporated a previous surrealist phase with the shelter drawings. The protective, enclosing mother figure of the finished *Madonna and Child* makes it one of his warmest, most renowned works.

Associated with Henry Moore in the group of British artists and architects known as Unit One, formed in 1933, was the sculptress Barbara Hepworth (1903–   ). The previous year she had also joined a circle of Parisian artists called Abstraction-Création, who practiced a style they designated *art concret*. This school of geometric abstraction was an outgrowth of the De Stijl movement and Russian constructivism, as transplanted to Paris. From an early naturalistic style, Barbara Hepworth has progressed toward a style of pure abstract shapes which reflects these international tendencies. Carving directly in wood and stone, she has shown in her severe pierced forms a special interest in the penetration of the sculptural mass by the surrounding space (Plate 187).

Another British sculptor who is of the same generation is Kenneth Armitage (1916–   ), who has produced many monumental cast-metal works. His philosophy of sculpture is perhaps best stated in his own words: "I like sculpture to look as if it had *happened,* and to express an idea as simply as possible. The moment when the work just sufficiently conveys the idea is the time also to finish, as further effort only neutralizes." His recurring theme has been these rudimentary figures, most often with several of them united in a single imposing bulk that has a suggestion of primitive religion or some primordial mystery about it (Plate 188).

Without doubt one of the most important American sculptors of this or any other period is Alexander Calder—engineer, illustrator, graphic artist, and inventor of the "mobile." Born in 1898, he first studied engineering, then drawing. At the age of twenty-eight, he went to Paris, where he made his first objects (sculpture is too misleading a term for these), which were a blend of cartoons and puppets. With these he put together a circus, with wire figures going round and round the ring, dancing and clowning. He used wire also to make a series of fascinating portraits that, when hung in a strong light, cast shadows of everchanging expressions on the wall. These simple animated caricatures set the course for his future experiments.

In 1931, he began to make much larger, abstract "sculptures" in which movement, though not yet actually present, was suggested by the forms. These elegant and lighthearted constructions, which Arp soon christened "stabiles," occupied Calder for some time. He then began to experiment with motorized versions, which the spectator could start and stop at will. But motors are an awkward artistic device, and Calder's major discovery, in 1932, was a way to create

189. *Mobile,* by Alexander Calder

191. *Sun Image I,* by Louise Nevelson

190. *The Great Spider,* by Alexander Calder

movement without such mechanical aids. Thus was born his distinctive art form, the "mobile."

Calder's mobiles, especially the early ones, look very simple. Their round or elegantly curved metal plates, which are either black or white or are painted in strong bright colors, hang on wires in flying formation in clusters and individually (Plate 189). When the slightest wind catches them, they bob and sway in diverting fashion, miraculously avoiding collisons by their carefully calculated arrangement. Frequently Calder placed them out of doors, in fields or in gardens, where like flowers and weathervanes they submit to the prevailing winds. Later he began to combine stable and mobile elements, using a framework to support the moving parts.

Calder was able to absorb what he needed from European artists—Miró, Mondrian, and Léger were his friends—and still reject the European view of what art itself was. Like Jackson Pollock (1912–1956), another very influential American artist, he found a way of freeing form and color from their European bonds. The mobile was in part a triumph because it was so novel and had to be considered and looked at in an entirely new way. Few modern artistic devices have so liberated form—regarded as something fixed within definite limits, that is—and in this respect Calder's achievement is enormous. Since World War II, he has divided his time between America and Europe, continuing to make mobiles and stabiles (Plate 190), and doing book illustrations and stage design as well.

Like the varied welded-metal techniques that have been an important innovation in modern sculpture, mixed-media constructions and assemblages of "ready-made" or "found" objects have made significant contributions to the art. Belonging to this category, yet very different from the machine-like precision of earlier constructivist sculpture, is the work of the American artist Louise Nevelson (1900–   ). Her large-scale constructions (Plate 191) are composed of a variety of hand-carved shapes and found items mounted in separate compartments

192. *Kouros,* by Isamu Noguchi

that are stacked together and painted all over in a uniform color (black, white, or gold). Her chief material is wood, but on occasion she has used the Plexiglas of the constructivists in her crowded arrangements.

Born of Japanese parents in Los Angeles, the American sculptor Isamu Noguchi (1904–   ) studied art first in New York and then went to Paris, where he studied with Constantin Brancusi in 1927–1928. In works such as his over-life-size marble *Kouros* ("Youth"; Plate 192), the influence of his master's pure, rigorously simplified forms is apparent, but in a highly personal and refined Oriental manner. Noguchi has been active also as a theatrical designer, notably for the modern dance productions of the Martha Graham troupe. Further evidence of his great versatility, may be found in his furniture and lamp designs, his work as a landscape architect, and his terracotta pieces, produced after he had traveled to Japan to study ceramic art.

Noteworthy among modern sculptors who work with welded metals, in the tradition of González and Gargallo, is the American Theodore Roszak (1907–   ). Accomplished in the use of blacksmith's tools and the acetylene torch, he devised a unique and complicated method of imposing surfaces of bronze and brass onto a solid steel base. His barbed organic shapes, agitated yet monumental in appearance, suggest some kind of fantastic marine or vegetable life (Plate 193).

Among the most important sculptors in Italy following World War II have been Giacomo Manzù (1908–   ) and Marino Marini (1901–   ).

In certain of his works, Manzù reveals himself as a very intellectual humorist in the uses of art. Besides being a masterful sculptor in a fairly traditional manner, he has made brilliant contributions to the discussion of what art is and what its proper

193. *Sea Sentinel,* by Theodore Roszak

subjects should be. During World War II he took shelter in the mountains of Italy, where he worked on, among other things, a series of Crucifixion scenes in which German soldiers played the part of the executioners. In 1949 he was chosen to make the fifth bronze door for St. Peter's in Rome, and has since done many commissions for churches as well as pursued his own highly personal experiments.

Manzù's series of seated and standing figures of cardinals (Plate 194) has brought him international fame. He has also done much work in the form of high-relief panels (Plate 195), which are very strongly pictorial in their placement of almost fully rounded figures against a plain background. These somehow bring to mind the great Italian medieval and Renaissance sculpted door panels, or even Roman classical reliefs.

194. *Cardinal,* by Giacomo Manzù

196. *Horse and Rider,*
by Marino Marini

195. *Artist and Model,*
by Giacomo Manzù

Marino Marini has enjoyed great popularity as well as critical recognition. His most successful and widely known efforts are his numerous horse-and-rider sculpture groups, which range from calmly monumental to highly abstract treatments of the theme (Plates 196, 197). He has also been extremely productive both as a painter and as a lithographer.

A third contemporary Italian sculptor of prominence is Mirko (family name, Basaldella; 1910–   ). His magical totemlike forms and finely engraved surface decoration call to mind the qualities of ancient Chinese ritual bronzes. He has completed several large commissions for war memorials, including the bronze gate for a park commemorating the massacre of several hundred Italian hostages by the Nazis during World War II at Fosse Ardeatine, outside Rome (Plate 198). In its intricate coiling patterns, this metal network suggests Oriental ideograms (pictorial symbols for words or ideas).

198. **Bronze gate, Fosse Ardeatine war memorial, outside Rome, by Mirko (Basaldella)**

197. *The Miracle,* by Marino Marini

European Painting: Between the Wars and After

GERMAN PATRIOTISM and German pride, so strong and assured before World War I, seemed to go up in smoke in the aftermath of the 1918 armistice. The artistic life of postwar Germany left its bitter record in the work of painters loosely grouped in a movement known as the "Neue Sachlichkeit" ("New Objectivity"). These painters were not interested, as were many artists elsewhere in Europe, in the new language of abstraction. They expressed their cynical views of official and social corruption in a war-tired country with a bitter, intensely felt realism.

George Grosz (1893–1959) was one of the originators of the Neue Sachlichkeit trend. His powerful satire, with its contempt for all tradition and social convention, was a reflection of his high-strung and violent personality.

Grosz started his career as an effectively vicious political cartoonist for the satirical magazines of his day. He became associated with the Dada movement in Berlin toward the end of World War I and produced savage pamphlets and paintings expressing his hatred of modern urban life. *The Funeral of the Poet Panizza* (Plate 199), for example, is a stinging social statement. The extreme distortions of perspective, the jumbled forms, the coffin, the skeleton, and the cookie-faced priest are all combined in an episode of social outrage. Grosz felt that an artist "should know how to present the outer appearance of things together with their inner content." He definitely succeeded in this aim. Following the war, he mercilessly chronicled the prevailing evils of

Germany, in some of the finest and fiercest pictorial satire ever created (Plate 200).

While Grosz may have set the general tone of German painting after the war, that country's most mature and noteworthy artist was Max Beckmann (1884–1950), who possessed enough individuality and personal integrity to cut a path of his own through these chaotic years. A product of the conservative Weimar Academy of Art, Beckman began his artistic career as a fairly typical expressionist. Following the example of Grosz, Beckmann went through a deliberately gruesome stage in which he painted scenes of frightening cruelty. He emerged from this phase and, learning from cubism, began to compose his pictures in a firmer, more disciplined manner. It was not until

200. *Metropolis,* **by George Grosz**

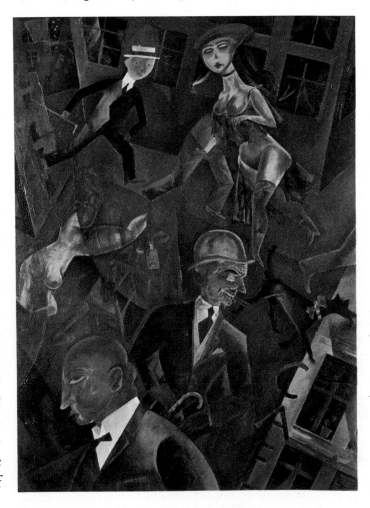

1925, however, that he came to full maturity as a painter, with a distinct contribution of his own.

Beckmann's later paintings, which often deal with the same themes as his earlier ones and have the same gloomy outlook, seem nevertheless calmer and more rooted in the artist's experience of the world (Plate 201). Beckmann then turned to great mythological and Biblical scenes, as in his *Perseus Triptych* (a triptych is a set of three related panel paintings). *The Departure* (Plate 202), though it seems intended to illustrate some ancient legend, also expresses feelings of exile and anxiety that were current in the Europe of the 1930's.

Otto Dix (1891–   ), unlike Beckmann later in his career, appears never to have recovered spiritually from the suffering and pain he had seen and undergone himself in trench warfare, nor from witnessing the misery of gassed and wounded soldiers. Because of their intensity, his feelings were difficult to communicate in terms of traditional painting. At first he experimented with making fantastic Dada collages out of ugly materials. These works are, as they were meant to be, shocking. He was still more successful when he turned to painting repulsive subjects such as corpse-littered yards in photographic detail. He even managed to endow a portrait of his parents with a strange sense of horror (Plate 203).

This hard, expressive realism of the postwar years was practiced in other countries as well. In Belgium, Constant Permeke (1886–1952) painted large, simplified figures of miners and peasants. Vigorously and dramatically presented, these are generally rendered in dark, burnt-looking colors. The drawing of the faces is quite original and manages to capture character (Plate 204). These massive figures are vaguely similar to

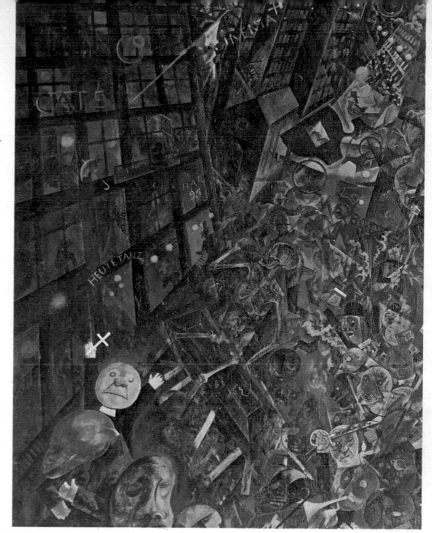

199. *The Funeral of the Poet Panizza,* by George Grosz

201. *Two Women,* by Max Beckmann

202. *The Departure*, by Max Beckmann

203. *The Artist's Parents*, by Otto Dix

204. *The Sailor Brothers*, by Constant Permeke

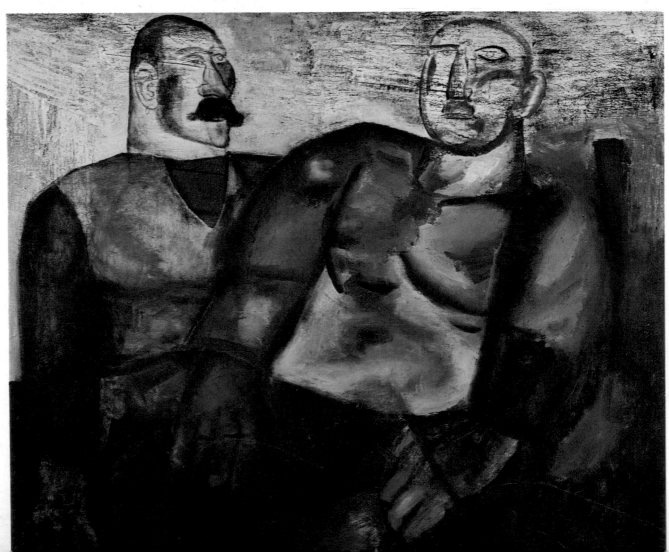

the sturdy people in the works of the French painter Marcel Gromaire (1892–   ), as seen in *The Lottery* (Plate 205).

A similar movement toward realism took place in Italy after World War I. This direction was most clearly seen in the magazine *Valori Plastici* ("Plastic Values"), the most influential publication concerning modern Italian painting. In particular, this magazine encouraged a return to the artistic forms of the great Italian tradition.

The painters who accepted the premises of *Valori Plastici* all too often produced monotonous uninspired paintings. But a few of them—Mario Sironi (1885–1961), in particular—managed to combine freshness with traditional qualities. In 1920, Sironi began a notable series of paintings depicting the dreary outskirts of industrial cities (Plate 206). Railway sidings, factories, and warehouses, painted in a limited range of browns,

205. *The Lottery,* by Marcel Gromaire

206. *The Suburb,* by Mario Sironi

208. *Evening Offering,* by Alfred Manessier

207. *Peonies,* by Filippo de Pisis

greenish grays, and dull whites, are combined in designs that have an unconventional strength.

This general movement of realism was known as Novecento Italiano ("Italian Twentieth Century"). The first exhibit of Novecento Italiano in 1926 made it quite obvious that one of the most talented of the group's members was Filippo de Pisis (1896–1956). De Pisis experimented with a number of modern styles, but none seemed to suit his own poetic and delicate temperament. He finally found what he was looking for on a trip to Paris in 1926. It was not the modern movement that excited him, but the shimmering color of the impressionists. From these painters he derived the gentle, lovely style to be seen in *Peonies* (Plate 207).

The French painter Alfred Manessier

(1911–) was one of the founding members of a group of abstract artists called "Peintres de tradition française" ("Painters in the French tradition"), which began its activity in 1941. Rather than the severe geometry of *art concret* and Purism, however, they chose to use freer abstract shapes in a style drawn from earlier cubist and even impressionist innovations in space and color—with a particular debt to Picasso. Characteristic of their art was its bright vibrant color, which added to the expressive power of the symbolic forms they created (Plate 208).

Born in St. Petersburg, Russia, Nicolas de Staël (1914–1955) was one of those twentieth-century artists who are loosely designated as members of the "school of Paris." Rather than representing a single unified style, this name has been given to numerous artists, both French and foreign, who have worked in Paris over several generations and who have displayed varying—though mostly abstract—stylistic tendencies. De Staël himself might be called one of the "second generation" of the school of Paris. To the Belgian theorist and art historian Michel Seuphor, he once identified his ideals as "Braque, Cézanne, and Matisse, and nobody else—nobody." The inspiration of these, one might say, "classic" masters of the modern movement is apparent in De Staël's bright-hued yet strongly architectural abstractions (Plate 209). In the last few years before his suicide at Antibes, he was again moving toward a more representational style and was also abandoning his brilliant palette in favor of more somber colors.

As in the United States, one of the important post-World War II trends in France has been the type of painting known as "abstract expressionism" or, more appropri-

209. *Le Lavandou,* by Nicolas de Staël

210. *The Financial and Economic System,* by Georges Mathieu

ately, "action painting." The terms used to describe the style in France are *art informel* and "tachism"—the latter being derived from the French word for "blot" or "stain." Those who paint in this style place strong emphasis on accidental effects that arise in the course of painting. In these impulsive, "unplanned" works, there is a stress on the very process or act of painting and whatever chance visual results it may lead to. (One should not, however, underestimate the amount of artistic control and choice involved in such "accidents.") Further, these artists determined to be completely "uninhibited by the past."

One of the most notable exponents of tachism is Georges Mathieu (1921–   ), who has demonstrated its wonderful and unpredictable possibilities by creating at least one of these action paintings extemporaneously before an audience. Both

he and his countryman Pierre Soulages (1919–   ) borrow heavily from Oriental ideograms for compositions rendered in a deliberately limited range of colors (Plates 210, 211, 216).

A French artist whose work very often resembles the art of children or that of the mentally disturbed is Jean Dubuffet (1901–   ), who has also spent time working in the United States. Originally a wine merchant and an occasional painter, Dubuffet has dedicated himself fully to art since 1942. In its comment on modern times, his *art brut* ("raw art") is a witty, sometimes bitter continuation of the surrealist and Dada spirit. In a style that combines thick-layered patches of brushwork with the slashing lines of caricature, there are also suggestions of primitive and barbarian art (Plate 212).

Dubuffet's pictures resemble nothing so

much as the walls of dilapidated buildings, pitted and scratched, covered with dirt, and scribbled all over. His attack on traditional values is at its best when he is being ironical. He paints cows or portraits in a childish manner that dignifies the cows and makes his portraits seem like animals. Earlier in his career Dubuffet used to paint a grotesque caricature first and only later add someone's name as a title. Resemblance to any living person might well have caused offense! This is clearly illustrated in his *Portrait of Edith Boissonnas* (Plate 213).

A former surgeon, the Italian Alberto Burri (1915–   ) exemplifies in his collage paintings the growing use of unconventional, often impermanent materials in contemporary art. Dissatisfied with the limitations and expressive qualities of traditional painting media, the modern artist has shown less and less concern with physical durability—with the ideal of "art for the ages." In coarsely textured compositions of pigment, burlap, and string (Plate 214), Burri carries this trend even farther by tearing gaping holes in his material. In more recent works he has experimented with effects achieved by applying plastics to the picture surface.

Three twentieth-century British painters have gained significant international reputations and influence: Francis Bacon (1910–   ), Graham Sutherland (1903–   ), and Ben Nicholson (1894–   ).

Both Bacon and Sutherland are loosely associated with a trend sometimes known as the "new realism," which has its roots in past English painting. Their work, clearly in the line of earlier visionary painters, often has strong literary allusions. Their personal outlook has taken quite different directions, however. In a style that has shown tinges of surrealism, metaphysical

211. *February 9,* by Pierre Soulages

212. *Rue Brise Elan,* by Jean Dubuffet

213. *Portrait of Edith Boissonnas,* by Jean Dubuffet

214. *Burlap and Red,* by Alberto Burri

216. *Composition,* by Pierre Soulages

215. *Portrait of Van Gongh,* by Francis Bacon

painting, and even *art informel,* Bacon has presented an essentially desperate and bleak view of the world (Plate 215). The pitiable condition of mankind that he observes produces feelings of helplessness and dread in the viewer.

Sutherland instead, perhaps as a result of his conversion to Catholicism, strikes a more affirmative note. He studied and first became known for engraving in the 1920's and 1930's. After a brief foray into surrealism, Sutherland arrived at the style for which he is best known in the years during and after World War II. Based on nature, the spiky forms characteristic of his mature semi-abstract style (Plate 217) also show the significant impression made upon him by Picasso's *Guernica.* In certain of his works, Sutherland has also given evidence of his close friendship with Francis Bacon. He generally chooses to depict strange or ghostly aspects of nature, natural features that are made to suggest disturbing human forms. Following World War II, he did a series of religious paintings that are powerful and vigorously modern within their basically representational style. Sutherland has also done some harsh and unconventional, yet realistic, portraits of famous sitters such as Winston Churchill and Somerset Maugham.

Slightly older than Bacon and Sutherland is Ben Nicholson, who paints in a quite different vein. Born into a family of artists, and married to the sculptress Barbara Hepworth in 1931, Nicholson has spent much of his later life in Cornwall. Not identified with the "new realism," he painted his first nonobjective (abstract) canvases as early as 1923. The main sources of his gentle, lyrical abstractions (Plate 218) are cubism, the Purism of Le Corbusier, and the neoplasticism of De Stijl and Mondrian, whom he knew in Paris during the 1930's.

217. *Thorn Trees,* by Graham Sutherland

218. *Still Life,* by Ben Nicholson

Painting: The American Scene

IN THE first years of the twentieth century, painting in the United States was largely dominated by impressionist and postimpressionist styles. But the quiet course of American painting was violently disturbed by three major exhibitions: a showing of Matisse in 1908, of Picasso in 1911, and, most important, of a large group of recent (and some nineteenth-century) European paintings in several American cities in 1913. This last was the famous Armory Show. Intended originally as an exhibit of contemporary American art, the show was stolen by the radically new European styles of cubism, expressionism, Fauvism, and Orphism. By comparison the American painters shown seemed unadventurous and hopelessly out-of-date.[1] The reaction of the general public ranged from astonishment to outrage, and the publicity—or more aptly, notoriety—attending the exhibition was enormous. In its aftermath, American art would never again be the same.

[1] Among the older mid- and late-nineteenth-century masters exhibited were Cézanne, Corot, Courbet, Daumier, Delacroix, Degas, Gauguin, Goya, Ingres, Manet, Monet, Munch, Pissarro, Puvis de Chavannes, Redon, Renoir, Seurat, Sisley, Toulouse-Lautrec, and Van Gogh.
More recent modern European artists shown included Archipenko, Bonnard, Brancusi, Braque, Delaunay, Derain, Duchamp, Dufy, Epstein, Kandinsky, Kirchner, La Fresnaye, Léger, Lehmbruck, Maillol, Marquet, Matisse, Pascin, Picabia, Picasso, Rodin, Rouault, Henri Rousseau, Villon, and Vuillard. (The selection of Matisse and Picasso works was particularly generous. However, the artist deliberately shown to the most extensive and greatest advantage was Odilon Redon.)
[2] Besides Sloan and Robert Henri, the other members of "The Eight"—all noteworthy names in American art—were: George Luks (1867–1933), William J. Glackens (1870–1938), Everett Shinn (1873–1953), Arthur B. Davies (1862–1928), Maurice Prendergast (1859–1924), and Ernest Lawson (1873–1939).

The American artist John Sloan (1871–1951) had been painting for many years before the Armory Show. He was a member of "The Eight," a group of artists who in 1908, fed up with smothering academic traditions, exhibited their "radical" realist paintings together.[2] They were among the first to take the ordinary street life of New York as a subject for painting, and their art was jeeringly nicknamed the "Ash Can school."

Sloan had been strongly influenced by Robert Henri (1865–1929), the leader of the group and the son of a fugitive from a Nebraska gunfight. Unlike Henri, Sloan quickly perceived that the work of Matisse, Brancusi, Kandinsky, and Duchamp held great lessons for American art. As he himself recalled, "I consciously began to be aware of the techniques of art. While I have made no abstract paintings, I have absorbed a great deal from the world of the ultra-modern." Therefore, although his *Haymarket* (Plate 219) reveals Sloan as a typical member of "The Eight," his paintings after the Armory Show became clearer in composition, and their structure obviously owed a great deal to the European examples.

George Bellows (1882–1925) was another painter who began with Robert Henri in New York, in 1904. His exceptional talent soon led to membership in the National Academy, and it was at this time that he, like Sloan, turned to a more structured kind of painting. In his case the example came from Jay Hambidge (1867–1924), who formulated the theory of "dynamic symmetry," a system of geometry underlying the main lines of the painting. Bellows followed Hambidge's theories of proportion and proclaimed that "there are no successful pictures without a geometric basis." Bellows be-

221. *Brooklyn Bridge,* by Joseph Stella

219. *Haymarket,* by John Sloan

came an extremely popular painter, especially for his sporting scenes. (He once thought of becoming a professional baseball player.) Basically a traditionalist, however, Bellows himself did little to advance the course of painting in America through his work (Plate 220).

This progress was accomplished by two artists, Joseph Stella (1880–1946) and John Marin (1870–1953), who wanted to readjust American traditions and bring them in line with contemporary developments in France and Italy.

Stella, an Italian immigrant, entered serious art after being trained as a commercial artist and illustrator for popular journals in New York. While working for *The Survey,* on a commission to draw steel mills, he decided that modern industrial subjects should form the subject matter of his art. He went back to Europe for four years (1908–1912), and there fully absorbed French cubism and the Orphism of Robert Delaunay. The interlocking circular mo-

220. *The Solitary Tenement,* by George Bellows

tion of Orphism can be seen in his *Brooklyn Bridge* (Plate 221) and in other American landscapes of the period. But it was the urgent speed of American urban life that really excited him, and in painting this he was even more influenced by futurism. "I was thrilled," he said, "to find America so rich with so many new motives [motifs] to be translated into a new art. Steel and electricity had created a new world."

John Marin, on the other hand, was less moved by modern city life than by the American landscape. Working largely in watercolor, he made delicate renderings of the natural world, which seem at first to owe a great deal to impressionism; these are more valuable, as works of art, than are his city scenes. Marin's free, sketchy technique became more and more abstract in his later years. Landscapes such as *Quoddy Head, Maine Coast* (Plate 222) were translated in terms of pure paint.

A group of regional painters, led by Thomas Hart Benton (1889–   ), Charles Burchfield (1893–1967), John Steuart Curry (1897–1946), and Grant Wood (1892–1942), devoted themselves to the presentation of American rural life. Grant Wood was in many ways typical of all of them. A trained artist, he chose to paint in a deliberate, self-consciously primitive style, continuing the early American tradition of sharp outlines and a hard, precise brushstroke. This was intensified after his visits to Flanders and Germany, where he developed his appreciation of the technique of Flemish and German late Gothic and early Renaissance painters. Wood's minute detail often has a toylike quality, and the background of his *American Gothic* (Plate 223) reminds one that he once earned his living as a maker of miniature model houses.

222. *Quoddy Head, Maine Coast,* by John Marin

223. *American Gothic,* by Grant Wood

Charles Burchfield was another regionalist who chose to paint the country he knew and loved. His art combines two important qualities: a feeling for the essential spirit of a particular landscape and an involvement with American history. *November Evening,* one of his finest works, is a poetic recollection of the days of Midwest pioneering. In its attention to domestic detail and sensitive treatment of woodwork and stone, Burchfield's *House of Mystery* (Plate 224) shows a certain resemblance to a painting by Edward Hopper (1882–1967), *House on the River Pamet.*

More characteristic of Hopper's work, however, is his *Night Café* (Plate 225), one of many rather melancholy paintings that arose from his personal experience with the loneliness of cities. Also trained by Robert Henri, Hopper was included in the Armory Show; afterward he did not change his style to any great extent but continued to paint in much the same way and with the same moody, slightly critical outlook. His paintings were created in his head, never from sketches or models.

Two American painters with a whole-hearted devotion to the cause of abstract painting were Arthur G. Dove (1880–1946) and Stuart Davis (1894–1967). Dove painted the first American abstracts. Though he always started from the natural appearance of things, he produced works, such as *Flour Mill Abstraction* (Plate 226), with no clear representational content.

Stuart Davis has the distinction of having introduced to American painting the areas of pop culture—advertising, jazz, the lights of Broadway—that have since become a major concern of the arts. Just as Dove foretells the abstract expressionism of the 1940's and 1950's, so too Davis sets a precedent for the Pop artists of the 1960's in his work (Plate 227).

224. *House of Mystery,* by Charles Burchfield

225. *Night Café,* by Edward Hopper

227. *The Paris Bit,* by Stuart Davis

226. *Flour Mill Abstraction,* by Arthur G. Dove

229. *Lily and the Sparrows,*
by Philip Evergood

"I took my place in the 1930's as part of the general uprising of social consciousness in art and literature," recollected the social realist Jack Levine (1915–   ). Like many other painters of the time, he was opposed alike to abstract art and to surrealism. Levine felt that he should try to "do something for the world." His paintings, lively and free in handling, expose corruption in American life with great satiric force (Plate 228).

Philip Evergood (1901–   ) has used a sharper line and simpler compositions, often with an element of fantasy, to make similar social statements. *Lily and the Sparrows* (Plate 229) is a surrealistic, personal work; in other, more public-minded paint-

228. *Welcome Home!* by Jack Levine

ings, he has sternly condemned such social ills as race prejudice and the poverty of American blacks in the midst of general affluence.

Another fine painter of protest is Ben Shahn (1898–1969). The son of Lithuanian Jewish parents, he arrived in the United States as an immigrant child. Raised in one of the poorest sections of Brooklyn, he was a lithographer's apprentice by day and studied at night classes after work. These classes eventually led him to New York University, and after that he made trips to France, Italy, Spain, and North Africa. Acutely conscious of developments in European painting, he felt uneasy about adapting them to his own style. An important decision was taken when he decided to give up all such attempts at changing his already formed artistic character. "' Here I am,' I said to myself, 'thirty-two years old, the son of a carpenter. I like stories and people. The French School is not for me.'"

It was at this stage that Shahn turned to social themes and began his famous series depicting the trial of Sacco and Vanzetti (Plate 230), two Italian anarchists who had been convicted of murder on an obviously trumped-up charge. The verdict, the result of anticommunist hysteria, was an insult to American justice and freedom. Horrified and angry, Shahn was so deeply moved that he felt, "Here I was living through another crucifixion. Here was something to paint!" In seven months he produced twenty-three gouache (tempera) paintings that show both restraint and dignity in their approach to the trial and ultimate execution. His somber theme is treated with compassion and frankness.

The Sacco and Vanzetti paintings, exhibited in New York, were much admired by the Mexican artist Diego Rivera, then

230. *The Passion of Sacco and Vanzetti,* by Ben Shahn

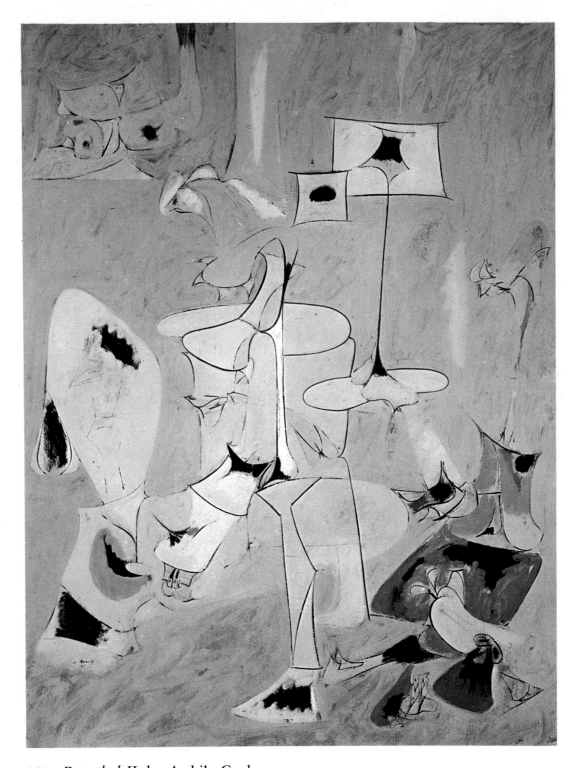

231. *Betrothal II,* by Arshile Gorky

232. *Removal of the Cards,* by Roberto Matta (Echaurren)

at work on his murals for Rockefeller Center. Rivera hired Shahn as an assistant, and Shahn's first mural commission, at a housing development for garment workers where he himself lived, shows unmistakable signs of Rivera's influence. Shahn's deep social sense mirrored many aspects of American life; it was not a distorting mirror, but rather a sharply critical one. Another series of his gouache paintings, which dealt with the persecuted trade unionist Tom Mooney, showed livelier color and a more complicated technique.

Among Americans who were most directly affected by contact with surrealism, Arshile Gorky (1904–1948) is an outstanding example. Most influenced at first by Picasso and Miró, he explored their discover-

ies and made them his own, always adding something personal to them. He eventually developed his own symbolic "language." His subdued color comes second to the drawing, which presents a succession of active areas and quiet spots. The viewer is left to use his imagination freely in interpreting Gorky's works. In *Betrothal II* (Plate 231) the drawing at various points suggests people, plants, and animals; but the ceremony in which these forms are engaged remains a puzzle.

Gorky was also affected by the Chilean painter Matta (Roberto Sebastian Matta Echaurren; 1912–   ), who had emigrated to France but also worked in the United States. The importance of Matta, who had formerly studied architecture with Le

233. *The Waiting Room,* by George Tooker

Corbusier in the 1930's, lies in the scale and complexity of his fantastic, abstract surrealist pictures and the way these draw the spectator into their space. Once the artist himself wrote, "What does it Matta if Matter is mad as a Hatta?" [Sic] The over-all effect of his pictures is that of some insane vision—as seen, for instance, in the half-insect, half-machine figures in *Removal of the Cards* (Plate 232).

The influence of surrealism on American artists was apparent in diverse ways. Among others so influenced were the group called "magic realists," exemplified in the paintings of George Tooker (1920–   ). Their painstakingly detailed realism was so strange

in its uniformly sharp focus and its dreamlike atmosphere that it took on surrealistic character. This curious effect derived from the magic realists' traits of unnaturally smooth surfaces, hypnotic expressions, and a kind of suspended movement throughout (Plate 233).

Throughout the 1930's and 1940's, the American art world was significantly affected by the arrival of European artists, many of them with already established reputations. Fleeing from a hostile political climate, they continued their careers in North America, enriching the artistic scene and often, in turn, being influenced by their new homeland. Among these was the painter

235. *The Dance*
by Robert Motherwell

234. *Emerald Isle,*
by Hans Hofmann

173

236. *Woman on a Bicycle,*
by Willem de Kooning

worked in an expressionist style. Gradually his expressionism became more abstract, and his late works are characterized by the vigorous brushwork and strong color of their free, intuitive compositions (Plate 234). His influence on other media has also been extensive.

Robert Motherwell (1915–   ), another of the American abstractionists, retains a firm clarity of outline in his free geometric shapes, usually painted in bold flat colors. In his compositions, there is a greater awareness of traditional rules of artistic balance; and in works such as *The Dance* (Plate 235), one finds a suggestion of the geometric purity and sensitive arrangement of Jean Arp's painted reliefs or of Matisse's colored-paper cutouts. And, in fact, Motherwell has often adopted the collage as a preferred medium.

The work of Willem de Kooning (1904–   ), like that of Gorky, reflects its heritage. He is able to absorb thoughtfully the achievements of earlier painters and continually experiments with elements from the artistic past. "There is," he has said, "a train track in the history of art that goes back to Mesopotamia." De Kooning's pictures are often frantic and violent. Violence is evident in the slashing quality of the brushwork itself (Plate 236). The emphasis on the act of painting as something having meaning and existence in itself—already described among the French tachists—has also characterized many New York artists in the post-World War II period. It is for this reason they are called "action painters." In De Kooning's work such "action" is apparent in the slurred paint, the broken line, and fragmented forms. His paintings, sometimes totally and sometimes only partly abstract, are often huge in scale.

The painting of large pictures was another

Hans Hofmann (1880–1966), who came from Germany in 1930.

Like other noted European emigrés, such as Archipenko and Moholy-Nagy, Hofmann was influential as a master teacher as well as a working artist. He became one of the prime forces in the development of abstract trends in the United States. During the early part of his career, in Germany, he had been in contact with Kandinsky and had

237. *Number 1,* by Jackson Pollock

trait common to most of the New York action painters. A big picture demands a response from the spectator. Some of the largest modern American paintings are those of the most famous action painter, Jackson Pollock. Some are sixteen feet long. Until about 1946 a more or less postcubist painter, Pollock combined certain cubist traditions with elements of Miró, Hans Hofmann, and the Mexican muralist José Clemente Orozco (1883–1949). From this blend of styles he created a completely new way of painting. He was a supreme master of line; in his greatest works of the late 1940's (Plate 237), the dribbled threads of line cross and recross the canvas in endless loops and swirls. The whole picture consists of an intricate network of lines.

Pollock's line differs from that of Gorky or Matta in that it is not an instrument of drawing, in the sense of descriptive representation. In conventional drawing, a line defines a form, a silhouette, or a division. Pollock's achievement was to free line from these traditional functions. Pollock used lines, blobs, and even occasional handprints to create a purely visual experience. These elements are never made to function as signs or symbols in his compositions; instead, they exist for their own sake. The content of the picture becomes the material form itself—neither more nor less (Plate 238).

The New York painters of the last several decades are often called "abstract expressionists," a term that is misleading for many of them. In Pollock's work, for instance, there is no perceptible "expression" whatsoever. Action paintings are not intended as *pictures* of things, but *as things* in themselves.

The work of Mark Tobey (1890–   ) illustrates another strand running through American painting: the influence of the Far East and Oriental culture. Tobey's pictures, like Pollock's, rely principally on line and have no particularly emphasized areas. While in the Orient, he found that he could "write" his feelings in layer upon layer of

238. *Gray over the Ocean*, by Jackson Pollock

239. *Forms Following Man,* by Mark Tobey

240. *Flight of Plover,* by Morris Graves

241. *The Scarecrow,* by Andrew Wyeth

endless calligraphy (the art of handwriting or penmanship; also, Oriental script). Back in America, during and after World War II, he made the "White Writing" series for which he is famous. This delicate style of calligraphic painting can be seen in *Forms Following Man* (Plate 239).

Another painter in this spirit is Morris Graves (1910–   ), who lives in solitude in the state of Washington. A visionary artist like Tobey, he has studied Oriental philosophies and religions in his search for the essence of life and nature. His paintings, most often of bird themes, clearly reflect this search and a mystique of nature, as can be seen in his breathtakingly expressive *Flight of Plover* (Plate 240).

Also a lover of nature, Andrew Wyeth (1917–   ) is technically the most accomplished present-day naturalistic painter in the United States. He has devoted his life to portraying the people and the countryside of his native eastern Pennsylvania. The son of a famous illustrator, Wyeth developed his meticulously realistic technique quite early. He applies his microscopic brushwork to haunting, mournful landscapes (Plate 241) and thoughtful portraits.

Mark Rothko (1903–   ), a master of color, passed through a phase of late surrealism before arriving at what is the purest, most simplified painting of the time in his distinctive abstract works (Plate 242). His great canvases of the late 1940's and 1950's are enormous, almost bare expanses of color in which subject matter has been reduced to a minimum. What remains is the glowing activity of two or three colors.

Franz Kline (1910–1962) was always drawing if necessary, on telephone books, menus, and letters—in an attempt to make things happen on paper to equal the live happenings around him. His powerful

242. *Red, White, and Brown,*
by Mark Rothko

black-and-white paintings (Plate 243), without the help of color, depend, as one critic admiringly remarked, solely on "the weighted brushstroke, the thick or thin, shiny or matte [dull] streaks of black and

244. *Small Rebus,* by Robert Rauschenberg

243. *Buttress,* by Franz Kline

white pigment. . . ." Kline's exhibition in 1950 announced "the last significant *new* extension of the radical abstract styles of the decade." Kline himself declared that the final test of painting is: "Does the emotion come across?" This must be the basis of his paintings—action and emotion. Even he refused to explain them, saying, "The first works in only black and white seemed related to figures, and I titled them as such. Later the results seemed to signify something—but difficult to give subject [or] name to, and at present I find it impossible to make a direct verbal statement about the paintings in white and black."

The New York artists of the postwar decade started yet another revolution in painting. In some respects, their innovations and achievements have proved to be dead ends, but not through any weakness of their own. It was simply that some of their art was unique and, therefore, showed no way forward as a consistent movement. In other ways, however, they opened new areas of advance for painters. Pollock's action painting was such a final triumph and proved so individual that his followers have seemed merely imitators, and few have successfully continued his work. The varieties of total abstraction established by Kline, Rothko, and Tobey, nevertheless, have become a basis from which artists both good and bad could proceed. An art so thoroughly stripped of all that was inessential could well absorb new subject matter and concerns—as indeed it has done, and will continue to do.

"A picture is more like the real world when it is made out of the real world." In these few words, Robert Rauschenberg (1925–   ) expresses a great deal of the contemporary artist's attitude toward the notion of art and toward the materials he uses. Viewing art as a "matter of just accepting whatever happens," he sees the act of creation as mainly a "collaboration" with the real external world. And what better way to depict this world than with actual items taken from it. Cubist and futurist collages had employed this technique, but usually for simple purposes of allusion—for instance, to suggest the life of the café or the spirit of music and the theater. In more recent work such as Rauschenberg's *Small Rebus* (Plate 244), however, these real components are put together with an eye to odd juxtapositions and a jarring removal from their original contexts. In his "combines" of pasted paper, bits of wood, photographs, oil paint on canvas, and other objects, Rauschenberg presents a fragmented view of reality that can be humorous and ironic or shocking and condemnatory in effect.

LIST OF ILLUSTRATIONS

150. *The Anti-Pope,* by Max Ernst. Peggy Guggenheim Collection, Venice.

151. *Large Composition,* by Joan Miró. Private collection, Milan.

152. *Man and Dog in Front of the Sun,* by Joan Miró. Öffentliche Kunstsammlung, Basel (Switzerland).

153. *Premonition of Civil War,* by Salvador Dali. Museum of Art, Philadelphia.

154. *Fear,* 1949 by Yves Tanguy. Oil on canvas 60 × 40″. Collection Whitney Museum of American Art, New York.

155. *Palace on a Promontory,* by Yves Tanguy. Peggy Guggenheim Collection, Venice.

156. *Configuration,* by Jean Arp. Öffentliche Kunstsammlung, Basel (Switzerland).

157. *Voice of the Winds,* by René Magritte. Peggy Guggenheim Collection, Venice.

158. *Perspective: Madame Récamier of Gérard,* by René Magritte. Private collection, Milan.

159. *Growth,* by Jean Arp. Solomon R. Guggenheim Museum, New York.

160. *Human Concretion,* by Jean Arp. Kunsthaus, Zurich.

161. *Table,* by Alberto Giacometti. Musée d'Art Moderne, Paris.

162. *The Piazza,* by Alberto Giacometti. Öffentliche Kunstsammlung, Basel (Switzerland).

163. *The Forest,* by Alberto Giacometti. Private collection, Paris.

164. *Beethoven on the Rocks,* by Emile Antoine Bourdelle. Bourdelle Museum, Paris.

165. *Hercules Aiming at the Stymphalian Birds,* by Emile Antoine Bourdelle. Metropolitan Museum of Art, New York.

166. *Renoir,* by Aristide Maillol. Landesmuseum, Hanover (Germany).

167. *Venus with a Necklace,* by Aristide Maillol. Kunsthaus, Zurich.

168. *Paulette,* by Charles Despiau. Musée d'Art Moderne, Paris.

169. *Man Singing,* by Ernst Barlach. Kunsthalle, Mannheim (Germany).

170. *Kneeling Woman,* by Wilhelm Lehmbruck. Museum of Modern Art, New York.

171. *The Maiastra,* by Constantin Brancusi. Peggy Guggenheim Collection, Venice.

172. *Sleeping Muse,* by Constantin Brancusi. Musée d'Art Moderne, Paris.

173. *The Rooster,* by Constantin Brancusi. Musée d'Art Moderne, Paris.

174. *Adam and Eve,* by Constantin Brancusi. Solomon R. Guggenheim Museum, New York.

175. *Construction in an Egg,* by Antoine Pevsner. Private collection, Paris.

176. *Woman Combing Her Hair,* by Julio González. Musée d'Art Moderne, Paris.

177. *Monserrat,* by Julio González. Stedelijk Museum, Amsterdam.

178. *Maternity,* by Pablo Gargallo. Private collection, Paris.

179. *Monument Commemorating the Destruction of Rotterdam,* by Ossip Zadkine. Rotterdam (outdoor).

180. *Sacrifice II,* 1948–52 bronze 49¼″ high by Jacques Lipchitz. Collection Whitney Museum of American Art, New York.

181. *Return of the Son,* by Jacques Lipchitz. Solomon R. Guggenheim Museum, New York.

182. *The Visitation,* by Sir Jacob Epstein. Tate Gallery, London.

183. *Selina,* by Sir Jacob Epstein. Brooklyn Museum, New York.

184. *Reclining Figure,* by Henry Moore. Tate Gallery, London.

185. *Warrior,* by Henry Moore. Kunsthalle, Mannheim (Germany).

186. *The Rocking Chair,* by Henry Moore. City Museum and Art Gallery, Birmingham (England).

187. *Two Figures (Menhir),* by Barbara Hepworth. Gimpel Sons Ltd., London.

188. *Two Standing Figures,* (1950), by Kenneth Armitage. Gimpel Sons Ltd., London.

189. *Mobile,* by Alexander Calder. Galleria Blu, Milan.

190. *The Great Spider,* by Alexander Calder. Öffentliche Kunstsammlung, Basel (Switzerland).

191. *Sun Image I,* by Louise Nevelson. Hannover Gallery, London.

192. *Kouros,* by Isamu Noguchi. Metropolitan Museum of Art—Fletcher Fund 1953, New York.

193. *Sea Sentinel,* Steel and bronze 105″ high 1956 by Theodore Roszak. Collection Whitney Museum of American Art, New York.

194. *Cardinal,* by Giacomo Manzù. Rhode Island School of Design, Providence.

195. *Artist and Model,* by Giacomo Manzù. Galleria Galatea, Turin.

196. *Horse and Rider,* by Marino Marini. Private collection, Turin.

197. *The Miracle,* by Marino Marini. Öffentliche Kunstsammlung, Basel (Switzerland).

198. Bronze gate, Fosse Ardeatine war memorial, outside Rome, by Mirko (Basaldella).

199. *The Funeral of the Poet Panizza,* by George Grosz. Staatsgalerie, Stuttgart, The Estate of George Grosz, Princeton, N.J.

200. *Metropolis,* by George Grosz. 1917 Museum of

Modern Art, New York, The Estate of George Grosz, Princeton, N.J.

201. *Two Women,* by Max Beckmann. Wallraf-Richartz Museum, Cologne (Germany).

202. *The Departure,* by Max Beckmann. Museum of Modern Art, New York.

203. *The Artist's Parents,* by Otto Dix. Öffentliche Kunstsammlung, Basel (Switzerland).

204. *The Sailor Brothers,* by Constant Permeke. Öffentliche Kunstsammlung, Basel (Switzerland).

205. *The Lottery,* by Marcel Gromaire. Musée d'Art Moderne, Paris.

206. *The Suburb,* by Mario Sironi. Private collection, Milan.

207. *Peonies,* by Filippo de Pisis. Private collection, Milan.

208. *Evening Offering,* by Alfred Manessier. Musée d'Art Moderne, Paris.

209. *Le Lavandou,* by Nicolas de Staël. Musée d'Art Moderne, Paris.

210. *The Financial and Economic System,* by Georges Mathieu. Private collection, Milan.

211. *February 9,* by Pierre Soulages. Kunsthaus, Zurich.

212. *Rue Brise Elan,* by Jean Dubuffet. Collection of the artist, Paris.

213. *Portrait of Edith Boissonnas,* by Jean Dubuffet. Galleria del Naviglio, Milan.

214. *Burlap and Red,* by Alberto Burri. Private collection, Milan.

215. *Portrait of Van Gough,* by Francis Bacon. Tate Gallery, London.

216. *Composition,* by Pierre Soulages. National Museum of Modern Art, Paris.

217. *Thorn Trees,* by Graham Sutherland. Albright-Knox Art Gallery, Buffalo, N.Y.

218. *Still Life,* by Ben Nicholson. Galleria Blu, Milan.

219. *Haymarket,* by John Sloan. The Brooklyn Museum, New York. Gift of Mrs. Harry Payne Whitney.

220. *The Solitary Tenement,* by George Bellows. National Gallery of Art, Washington, D.C. Gift of Chester Dale.

221. *Brooklyn Bridge, Variations on an old theme* 1939 by Joseph Stella. Oil on canvas 70 × 42″. Collection Whitney Museum of American Art, New York.

222. *Quoddy Head, Maine Coast,* by John Marin. Phillips Collection, Washington, D.C.

223. *American Gothic,* 1930 by Grant Wood. Courtesy of the Art Institute, Chicago.

224. *House of Mystery,* by Charles Burchfield. The Art Institute, Chicago.

225. *Night Café,* by Edward Hopper. The Art Institute, Chicago.

226. *Flour Mill Abstraction,* by Arthur G. Dove. Phillips Collection, Washington, D.C.

227. *The Paris Bit* 1959, by Stuart Davis. Oil on canvas 46 × 60″. Collection Whitney Museum of American Art, New York.

228. *Welcome Home!* by Jack Levine. Brooklyn Museum New York.

229. *Lily and the Sparrows,* 1939 Oil on composition board 30 × 49″, by Philip Evergood. Collection Whitney Museum of American Art, New York.

230. *The Passion of Sacco and Vanzetti,* 1931–32 From the series of 23 paintings of Sacco–vanzetti Tempra on canvas 84½ × 48″, by Ben Shahn. Collection Whitney Museum of American Art, New York. By courtesy of Kennedy Galleries.

231. *Betrothal II,* by Arshile Gorky. 1947 Oil on canvan 50¾ × 38″. Collection Whitney Museum of American Art, New York.

232. *Removal of the Cards,* by Roberto Matta (Echaurren). Galerie du Dragon, Paris.

233. *The Waiting Room,* by George Tooker. Johnson Collection, Museum of Art, Philadelphia.

234. *Emerald Isle,* 1959 by Hans Hofmann. Smithsonian Institute, Washington, D.C.

235. *The Dance,* by Robert Motherwell. Metropolitan Museum of Art, New York.

236. *Woman on a Bicycle,* 1952–53 Oil on canvas 76½ × 49″. by Willem de Kooning. Collection Whitney Museum of American Art, New York.

237. *Number 1,* by Jackson Pollock. Museum of Modern Art, New York.

238. *Gray over the Ocean,* by Jackson Pollock. Solomon R. Guggenheim Museum, New York.

239. *Forms Following Man,* by Mark Tobey. Fuller Collection, Art Museum, Seattle.

240. *Flight of Plover,* 1955 by Morris Graves. Oil on composition board 36 × 48″. Collection Whitney Museum of American Art, New York.

241. *The Scarecrow,* by Andrew Wyeth. Johnson Collection, Museum of Art, Philadelphia.

242. *Red, White, and Brown,* by Mark Rothko. Öffentliche Kunstsammlung, Basel (Switzerland).

243. *Buttress,* by Franz Kline. Private collection, Varese (Italy).

244. *Small Rebus,* by Robert Rauschenberg. Private collection, Varese (Italy).